CONCILIUM

Religion in the Eighties

CONCILIUM

Concilium 204 (4/1989): Dogma

CONCILIUM

List of Members

Advisory Committee: Dogma

WORLD CATECHISM OR INCULTURATION?

Edited by
Johann-Baptist Metz
and
Edward Schillebeeckx

English Language Editor
Philip Hillyer

T & T CLARK LTD
Edinburgh

August 1989
ISBN: 0 567 30084 6

ISSN: 0010-5236

Typeset by C. R. Barber & Partners (Highlands) Ltd, Fort William
Printed by Page Brothers (Norwich) Ltd

Concilium: Published February, April, June, August, October, December.
Subscriptions 1989: UK: £29.95 (including postage and packing); USA: US$49.95
(including air mail postage and packing); Canada: Canadian$64.95 (including air mail
postage and packing); other countries: £29.95 (including postage and packing).

Contents

International Theological Conference

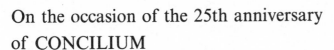

On the occasion of the 25th anniversary
of CONCILIUM

from September 9–14, 1990, at the University of Leuven

THEME: ON THE THRESHOLD OF THE THIRD MILLENIUM

THE THEME of the conference is in three sections. The first will review the recent past of church and world and evaluate both positive and negative aspects.
Speakers: E. Schüssler Fiorenza and C. Duquoc

A more analytical and descriptive second section deals with the choice for life or death.
Speakers: J. Moltmann and D. Tracy

The third section especially involves the religious and theological manner of speaking about God and the coming kingdom of God as salvation and well-being of and for mankind.
Speakers: H. Küng and G. Guttiérrez

The lectures will be printed in advance in February 1990 in a special conference issue of CONCILIUM. This will allow emphasis during the actual conference to fall on group discussion and plenary meetings.

With this announcement CONCILIUM invites all those interested in the conference to take part in it as observers.

We would welcome your applications addressed to the General Secretariat of CONCILIUM, c/o Mrs. E. Duindam-Deckers, Prins Bernardstraat 2, 6521 AB Nijmegen, The Netherlands.

We can also supply information about inexpensive lodgings.

The registration fee for the conference is US $15.00

We would like to request that all Faculties and Institutes pin up a notice about this conference in a place appropriate to informing any interested visitors about it. For this you can use a copy (enlarged) of the Announcement.

CONCILIUM 204 Special Column

Gregory Baum

The Church Against Itself

WHILE POWERFUL forces in Rome are presently creating a more authoritarian church organisation and try to eliminate the vestiges of democracy from church life, recent papal social teaching, in an extraordinary evolution, has come to recognise democratic participation as a requirement of the divine order and the natural law.

The key concept used in papal teaching, especially in Laborem exercens *(1981) and* Sollicitudo rei socialis *(1987), is the human being as 'subject.' Humans are meant to be 'subjects,' i.e. responsible agents of their society and all institutions to which they belong. Governments must respect what John Paul II calls 'the subjectivity' of its people. People have the right to participate in the decisions that affect their lives. Even measures taken by government to protect the common good can claim to be ethical only if the subjectivity of the people has been respected. People are 'subjects' individually and collectively. From reflecting on their very nature, we must affirm the personal right of responsible participation and the collective right of cultural and political self-determination.*

According to papal teaching, workers are meant to be the subject, not the 'object' of production. Workers are entitled to share in the decisions that deal with the organisation of labour and the use of the products of their hands. Both capitalism and communism deprive workers of this human right. Because of the alienation inflicted on workers, they could become the principal agent of social transformation in East and West. To promote this struggle, Laborem exercens *calls for 'the solidarity of labour and with labour.' (n. 8).*

Recognising the destiny of people to become the subject of their society and its institutions, Sollicitudo rei socialis *(n. 15) offers a trenchant critique of authoritarian rule. Probably thinking of his own country, John Paul II has this to say. 'No social group—for example, a political party—has the right to usurp the role of sole leader, since this brings about the destruction of the true subjectivity of society and of the individual citizens, as happens in every form of totalitarianism. In this situation the individual and the people become "objects", despite all the declarations to the contrary.'*

John Paul II does not use the word 'democracy'. Perhaps it sounds too Western to him, too closely linked to liberal political theory. What the Pope calls for is a participatory society. His choice of vocabulary here is significant. Modern democracy is after all connected with the theory of popular sovereignty and hence does not apply to the Church founded on God's empowerment. But the human destiny to be 'subject', to be a responsible, participating agent, must be respected by all institutions, including the Church.

Still speaking of his own country, John Paul II defends 'the right to economic initiative', a right largely denied in Poland, while being gradually restored in China and other socialist countries. We note that this right is not understood as a justification of the free enterprise system. The encyclical clearly denounces the flaws of Marxist collectivism and liberal capitalism. In an extraordinary passage, John Paul II offers a critique of the over-bureaucratisation of the Polish economy, a critique that applies to all forms of bureaucracy that do not respect the subjectivity of the people.

> *Experience shows that the denial of the right to economic initiative diminishes or in practice absolutely destroys the spirit of initiative, that is to say the creative subjectivity of the citizens ... In place of creative initiative there appears passivity, dependence and submission to the bureaucratic apparatus which is the only 'ordering' and 'decision-making' body—if not also the owner—of all the goods and the means of production, puts everyone in a position of absolute dependence, which is similar to the traditional dependence of the worker-proletariat in capitalist society. This provokes a sense of frustration or desperation and predisposes people to opt out of national life, impelling many to emigrate or to favour a form of psychological immigration (n. 15).*

The life of any large society calls for organisation, administration, and bureaucracy. But when a bureacratic apparatus defines itself as the sole 'ordering' and 'decision-making' body, it destroys creative initiative, produces passivity and submission, and generates a sense of frustration that predisposes people to opt out of the organisation altogether.

We have then the curious contradiction that at the very time the Vatican tries to return to centralisation, control and authoritarian rule, the Church's magisterium affirms the divinely-grounded human destiny to be 'the subject' of society and its institutions. The efforts of the Vatican to define itself as the sole 'ordering' and 'decision-making' body in the Church is judged by the Church's official teaching. Since the Church is a public sign and symbol, the refusal to follow its own teaching greatly weakens the power of its message.

Note that this Special Column, like others in this series, is written under the sole responsibility of the author.

Dietmar Mieth

Nostalgia

LAST CENTURY, the Pope's personal physician, on examining the Swiss Guard, diagnosed a psychosomatic illness which he called 'nostalgia'. The longing to be secure in the place of one's origin is probably best caught in German by the word 'Heimweh' (homesickness). But the word nostalgia has a greater reach today. 'Spatial' longing has been replaced by 'temporal' longing: the longing for a past and the desire to renew it or re-experience it.

The word nostalgia as an expression and a diagnosis of our present time has, meanwhile, extended in all possible directions, and, powered by its inflationary use, has brought under its claim to dominance many phenomena which look alike but are not perhaps identical. This makes defining it difficult. It is like spilling a glass of water which saturates more than one would have thought beforehand, or like the mercury from a broken thermometer which rolls away in all directions and breaks up into ever smaller globules.

At the annual gathering of the Concilium directorate, after Whit 1989, I had the opportunity to ask many of my learned and astute colleagues, both men and women, what phenomena came under this expression 'nostalgia' and how these should be properly described. Within this gathering I was also able to question different generations. At first I was surprised that youth too can be 'nostalgic', even if it is not a question of the memory of a past one has experienced oneself, but rather of the rediscovery and renewal of traditions which awaken in young people the longing to experience something which they sense was important to people long before their own generation. As examples in the area of religion, Gregorian Chant and monks praying at the appointed nocturnal hours were mentioned. In the secular world, it is more the longing to appropriate the experiences of an earlier generation (e.g. the Fifties) that is important, but also a nostalgia, on the one hand, for the 'new departures' in modern society and, on the other hand, against the secured 'orders' in bourgeois society. In the world (and in that of the university as well) it is the longing for the feeling of being secure that one observes, rather than the longing for the feeling of being 'free' in a new way. In this there is a generation gap, because the middle generation, shaped by its experiences around the time of the 'new departures' of the Sixties, feels in a totally different way from the 'post-modern' generation which is characterised by its love of difference and of security in small groups, once described by the writer Botho Strauss as 'nests of solidarity'. In the German universities the colours of the student societies can be seen again, and many a professor has his eye on the old robes which in many places have been hanging in the cupboard since 1968. The 'musty smell' has not vanished with the years and an air of resignation hangs over the futility of replacing old worlds of symbols with new ones. For symbols cannot either be dispensed with nor can they be enforced.

Differentiating between people's nostalgic states of mind, in the sense of discretio spiritum, brings out, in the first instance, components which are above suspicion and indeed even productive. The longing for a 'lost time' (Marcel Proust), the transforming appropriation of the past by the culture of memory, the claim of unfulfilled 'dreams of childhood' (J.-B. Metz) and the continuing effect of 'model childhoods' (Christa Wolf)—all that is basically timeless, even if it is always, so to speak, new in its time. All can share in it. The evocation of one's own experience is replaced by the (often commercial!) evocation in creative narrative form of the experience of others. Am I nostalgic because I idealise my remembered experience and its concomitant feelings, or am I nostalgic because I have a longing for that other which I did not undergo, did not experience, but to which others testify with their narratives? There is obviously spontaneous nostalgia of the first kind and transmitted or acquired nostalgia of the second kind.

It is not a little tempting to develop a nostalgia for nostalgia, because the feelings of a romanticising longing bound up with it are enjoyable as both pleasure and pain. Late Romantic poetry is full of it: 'and my soul stretched out/wide its wings' (Joseph von Eichendorff). But our critical consciousness should not let itself be completely dragged down into the whirlpool of the pleasurable enjoyment of the difference between feelings, otherwise the temptation to join in uncritical allegiance is far too great. A simple critical distinction has to be made: as long as nostalgia does not postpone man's longing for both freedom and security by onesidedly favouring security at the expense of freedom, that is, as long as it is a balanced nostalgia, a nostalgia in equilibrium, then it will also provide a critical impulse, a stimulus to set enlightenment in motion, to lead one to commitment and not escape. But if nostalgia turns completely into the longing for the feeling of being secure, *it no longer contains the component of dangerous memory, only the desire to reanimate old styles of living or to rebuild the walls of order, of paternalistic authorities, of unquestioning (and therefore questionable) solidarities. This nostalgia is the 'fruitful womb' (Bert Brecht) of the 'resistible rise' of old myths, befogging the mind and stealing from the heart the 'exactness of feeling' (Robert Musil).*

Gabriel Marquez's book Love in the Time of Cholera *is a good example of this differentiation of minds. The longing for the completely other aspect of love, namely for the faithfulness to love as adventure, a longing spontaneously felt by the older people, transmitted second hand to the younger ones, this longing is repeatedly refracted by irony and so creates a consciousness which is at once both nostalgic and critical. The ethical responsibility of nostalgia can only be guaranteed by irony and humour. It is not wrong to feel and dream the difference between various times. It is not wrong to revel with the poets in the unresolved balance of longing and satire. But to make an escape, organised by a powerful nostalgia for security, to the coat-tails of the past and into the paternalistic bosom of idealising structuralised order, that is wrong. Wherever nostalgia becomes the accomplice of disentitlement, one must confront it not only with the power of reason but also with the dream of new departures to freedom, whether it be in the Churches or in the full social glare of the market-place.*

There is, therefore, a 'naive', an 'active' and an 'ironic' nostalgia. 'Naive' nostalgia encompasses the biographical or the historic past, by cultivating it just as much as its concomitant feelings. 'Active' nostalgia experiments with the return of what has been. It is ambiguous because the past can be the womb of both what is good and what is bad. So there is an exodus-nostalgia and an ordo-nostalgia. 'Ironic' nostalgia tries to clarify in a critical way feelings of wistfulness; it is a nostalgia which is enlightened and rational, but in the sense that it does not give up on the feelings, instead it elevates them into the clarifying light of reason. Robert Musil's desire for a 'general-secretariat for exactness and the soul' is, in this sense, both ironic and creative. The nostalgia of our time has arisen as a counterbalance to rationality and instrumentalisation, and also as a counterbalance to the authority of freedom. This ambiguity urges us to be careful, urges us to test dreams against realities and the longing for security in its totalitarian consequences.

Translated by Gordon Wood

Note that this Special Column, like others in this series, is written under the sole responsibility of the author.

WORLD CATECHISM
OR INCULTURATION?

Editorial

THE TOPIC discussed in this *Concilium* is intimately related to the theme of the last two Dogma issues. In 1985 our subject was the magisterium of the faithful, and in 1987 the theme was orthodoxy and heterodoxy. Now we are concerned with unity and plurality, with special reference to the present debate in the Church throughout the world about a universal catechism and/or inculturation.

I

The Second Extraordinary Synod of Bishops approved a final document on 9 December 1985. Referring to the 'sources from which the Church lives', the Synod stated: 'Without doubt there is a unanimous desire for a catechism or compendium of the entire teaching of the Catholic Church regarding faith and morals, as a yardstick, so to speak, for the catechisms or compendia which are to be produced in different areas. The exposition must have a biblical and liturgical emphasis, be doctrinally correct, and also be appropriate to the way in which life is perceived by the faithful today.'

On the one hand, we have the remarks on the foregoing of the special secretary to the Synod: 'This proposal in no way emanated from the Curia. It was not a product of the centralistic mind. The initial impulse came from the periphery, from the Third-World churches. Admittedly, the suggestion was then taken up by the European and US bishops. When the Synod, for obvious reasons, did not immediately respond, the proposal was put forward once again by several language groups' (see Walter Kasper, on the Extraordinary Synod in *Zukunft aus der Kraft des Konzils*).

On the other hand, it is no secret that in the nineteen-seventies Cardinals Oddi and Ratzinger advocated a universal or world catechism. Cardinal

3

Oddi went so far as to prepare a provisional text which was unanimously rejected by the International Catechetical Commission. Cardinal Ratzinger for his part spoke out for a world catechism at the Lyons and Paris conferences. Therefore the suggestion that the idea of a catechism for the whole Church came not from the Curia but from the Third World is scarcely the whole truth.

To be sure, this plan for a world catechism does not conceal some kind of intended 'indoctrination'. It is an attempt to take account of the new pluralist aspect of the universal Church in the area of catechesis and the propagation of faith. Accordingly fundamental problems are touched on which also, and in particular, have to do with dogmatic theology. Hence the synodal text suggests that there is something like an inalienable 'deposit' of doctrine regarding faith and morals which remains 'essentially' unaffected by cultural history and diversification. Moreover, the text appears to insist on a 'quantitative' wealth of doctrinal content, without mentioning the *hierarchia veritatum*, or hierarchy of truths.

What is more, is this world catechism intended as an 'instrument of instruction' or as a 'document of faith'? Then we must ask whether in all cultures a 'catechism as an instrument of instruction' is necessarily a possible means of imparting and transmitting the faith. How does this projected world catechism look in the light of the task of an authentic inculturation which the Council enjoined on us?

The synodal text also betrays the opinion that the crisis of religion is primarily doctrinal and not above all a crisis of Christian individuals and of institutions and their praxis. Clearly we then touch on the question of a correct diagnosis of the present critical situation, and not least of all on the question how we are to assess the so-called crisis of transmission of faith and how it is to be dealt with in a culturally polycentric universal Church.

II

This *Concilium* examines the question 'World catechism or inculturation?' in three thematic areas. Throughout these three sections, there are clear critical queries about the projected world catechism.

The first group is concerned with the project of a world catechism as explained and criteriologically defined in the synodal text. Brodeur makes reservations in regard to the four criteria set forth in the synodal text ('The exposition must have a biblical and liturgical emphasis, be doctrinally correct, and also be appropriate to the way in which life is perceived by the faithful today'). He discerns in this an excessive concern with preservation, and an excessively defensive ideology of security. On the other hand, he stresses the significance of proclamation as part of the task of a missionary enterprise.

Joncheray offers critical observations on the catechism's assumption that there is a homogeneous catechetical situation in all countries, which is clearly not the case. He emphasises the significance of the way in which ecclesiastical belief is constituted on 'a second person plural basis' which ought not to be suddenly erased by catechesis and catechisms.

Tracy warns of the danger of introducing a Eurocentric concept of the 'world' into such a catechism. He shows that universality is always mediated through particularity, and in this respect he opposes the notion of a deposit of faith transcending history and culture and notionally precedent to all inculturation.

A second thematic group concentrates on actual ecclesial and theological experience with catechisms, above all in the context of the currently urgent question of the imparting and transmission of faith. In his article Marthaler first offers a short history of the literary genre of 'catechism' since the sixteenth century, and shows clearly the way criticism of catechisms by the church historian Claude Fleury (1640–1723) was even then fundamentally the same as present-day criticism of current projects.

As against a certain euphoric tendency to expect from a universal catechism a cut and dried solution to the crisis over transmitting the faith in family and parish, Werbick recalls how essential actual witness through practice is for all proclamation, and refers to the necessity and significance of a form of argument which aims at understanding, and which tries to offer an appropriate situational, cultural and intellectual answer to objections to specific elements of faith.

Häring connects experience of the so-called 'short-formulas of faith' with the projected world catechism, and thus discovers criteria and boundaries for expectations of such a catechetical project. Discussion of the short-formulas showed how important is orientation to individuals and those concerned in this mode of transmission of faith. Therefore Häring argues for more prudence and sobriety in claims for a universal catechetical project.

The third section of this issue then expressly and amply extends the theme to the question of inculturation. Metz in his article tackles the new association of 'unity and diversity' in its repercussions on Church and theology on the way to a culturally polycentric universal Church. He concentrates on problems with the idea of a Christianity which is pre-existent to culture and history and somehow 'plain', and which is wrapped round individual cultures 'like a garment'. He shows how a cultural polycentrism can succeed, precisely if the history of the origins of the European West is not simply laid aside.

Alberich is concerned exclusively with the theoretical difficulties between the project of a world catechism and the understanding of inculturation which prevailed at the most recent Council. He raises the critical point of how a universal catechism can help to promote the inner differentiation in the life of the Church and of faith required by inculturation. His proposal aims at a gradually established form of 'unity through complementarity'.

Rottländer's article is about the understanding of the world prevalent in discussion of the universal catechism and inculturation. Whereas the inculturation debate presupposes a multiplicity of worlds, the universal catechism project is in danger of prescinding from one world of the West, which is currently undergoing an increasing levelling down and de-differentiation. That one world threatens the identity and dignity of those worlds which in a polycultural Christianity have to be nurtured, protected and supported in solidarity.

In the last article in this issue, Benda shows how in the present situation of Church and world the universal catechism project and the ecumenical project for the 'conciliar process for justice, peace and the preservation of creation', are related – at least indirectly – and can profit from one another.

Johann-Baptist Metz
Edward Schillebeeckx

Translated by J. G. Cumming

PART I

Critical Analysis and Assessment

Raymond Brodeur

Producing a Catechism: A Matter of Principle

THE BISHOPS who took part in the second Extraordinary Synod put forward the suggestion, in their document dated 9 December 1985, of drawing up 'a catechism or overall exposition of the whole of Catholic teaching dealing with both faith and morals, which would serve as a point of reference for catechisms or overall expositions drawn up in various countries'. They defined their purpose in these terms: 'Doctrine should be presented in a biblical and liturgical manner, presenting an integral doctrine but at the same time one adapted to present-day Christian life.'

Is this proposal appealing to a general principle which would have a direct influence on the 'presentation of doctrine'? Would this tend to produce a work which aimed to establish a pluriform dynamic in which the various poles—'biblical and liturgical ... presenting an integral doctrine but at the same time one adapted to present-day Christian life'—could exist and make sense only in a relationship of mutual tension? Or should the proposal rather be understood as appealing to four separate principles, to be juxtaposed and added on to one another so as eventually to provide a thesaurus of 'what must be believed'? Even if the use of the word 'catechism' tends to indicate that it is the second course they had in mind, both deserve consideration.

1. Four separate principles

To deal with the second course first: Herbert Vorgrimler courageously initiated criticism of these four principles in his article 'The Adventure of a

New Catechism' in *Concilium* 192 (1987). As a prelude to making them comprehensible, however, he suggested the need for a hermeneutic of fundamental theology, which had to come before any other hermeneutic, whose aim would be to establish, in a manner intelligible to the modern world, what is meant by the word of God, revelation, hearing and understanding the word of God. Such a hermeneutic, according to Vorgrimler, would consist essentially in linking possible and actual experiences of God in the present with memories of God attested in the message of the Church. One might add that it would consist in re-reading, on a daily basis, the God who continues to reveal himself, and in comparing these readings with those spread through the history of the Church.

Present-day research into the way catechisms have been produced in different cultures, though, reveals the lack of any hermeneutic in the sense defined by Vorgrimler.[1] In the context of European Christendom which provided the setting for the composition of modern catechisms, the principles underlying their production were, in general terms, of two sorts: theological and pedagogical. On the theological level, they had to limit themselves to setting out only those truths generally accepted by the whole Catholic Church as fundamental to faith. In pedagogical terms, care was taken to simplify the language so that children could understand it. In such a context, who could even have dreamed of asking what really happened when people set out to produce such a work? Each author, individual or group, could only tackle a narrowly-defined task.[2]

This culture was marked by the importance given to rhetoric, defined by treatises *De Rhetorica* as 'the art of convincing'. In such a setting, the various elements preceding the production, diffusion and reception of catechisms functioned alongside one another, leaving little room for basic examination of principles. Such productions, aimed at a wide public, had the effect of consolidating socio-cultures. Their other effect was in some way to fix people in their historicity, to congeal their personal history—the evolution of their mentality and ideologies—in foundations that were then difficult to shift.

Such catechisms say far more about those who conceive them and their purposes than they do about those for whom they are destined. Any sort of discourse, in fact, 'is never written on a blank sheet. When it is established, this can only be done in a field already saturated by others'.[3] A catechism is, from this point of view, a discourse on its own. It finds its niche in the meeting-point between what Charles Wackenheim has called the three worlds that often rub shoulders without meeting: that of the churches (or the religions, we might rather say today), that of culture and learning, and that of civil, economic and political society.[4] During the course of ecclesial catechesis, this discourse with its characteristic genre and form has come, not to take the place of, but to approximate to the discourses of mission and evangelisation (those that proclaim the Kerygma), those of preaching and the homily (developing the understanding of faith in life), those of dogma, morals, canon law and liturgy (developing the intelligence of faith). In this respect, a catechism can be biblical, but cannot be the Bible; liturgical, without being the liturgy; teach holy doctrine, without being a dogmatic treatise; adapted to the outlook of modern life, without taking the place of ethical discourse.

Such texts, emanating from such high authority and aimed at such a wide public, are subject to major constraints. Seeking to teach the whole world, starting with children, without sacrificing anything of the essentials of the discourses concerned, they impose choices of authority without which no printed production is possible. The *corpus* of catechisms, as it took shape in the discursive space marked out by the Reformation/Counter-Reformation discourse doublet, therefore imposes new game plans deriving from the nature of writings destined for a wide public.

Producing a catechism becomes the prime sphere in which authority plays a dual highly magisterial role: teaching the mass of the faithful, but also, and perhaps above all, slowing down other doers of theological discourse. Through a dynamic phenomenon which linguisticians call intertextuality, no text exists on its own, unless it is out of circulation and without an audience. There is no way of 'making' a catechism without setting in motion, at least implicitly, an evocation of all the other limit texts mentioned above. This intertextuality therefore both makes possible and effects recourse to a reservoir of texts with which this particular text is associated, sometimes in a surprising manner. In this respect, it corroborates Marc Angenot's thesis that:

> In every society, the interaction of discourses, the interests that uphold them and the need to 'think' historical novelties according to the rules, end up by producing a hegemony constantly being re-made, which overall determines a large part of what is *thinkable/sayable* and which, above all, deprives the unthinkable—the *noch-nicht gedachtes*, to adapt Ernst Bloch—of means of expression, even though it in no way corresponds to the inexistant or chimerical.[5]

From the viewpoint of a history of socio-culture, freeing a catechism of the religious anthropology that provided its substratum renders it 'living'. As Bernard Plongeron has remarked, one then discovers that the skeleton of any catechism, destined to structure time, space, the world of imagination and action, is ultimately articulated in relation to the struggles of a Western world perpetually torn between two anthropological approaches: the Pelagian view of human fate based on the freedom of creatures made in the image of God, and the Augustinian view of humankind marked by the wound of original sin and at the end of a Promethean adventure which began in the Garden of Eden. In its dogmatic form, Plongeron concludes, this catechetical product cannot allow itself to open up a debate which concerns more than human life itself: humankind's eternal salvation.[6] The same can be said of a catechism in its scriptural, liturgical and moral form.

The ultimate verification of the rightness of a discourse, and of that of the reservoir of texts to which it belongs, is made when practically all those belonging to a particular society draw the same meaning from this reservoir. There is no doubt that at the time of the Reformation and Counter-Reformation, the catechism was largely responsible for defining the boundaries of what was 'thinkable'. When social consensus breaks down in both its recognition of the reservoir of texts and the meaning it assigns to a particular text, culture is in crisis.

In the case that concerns us here, we can suspect that Vatican II came at a time of acute cultural crisis and, as Claude Geffré says in his course on the theology of non-Christian religions,[7] marks a radically new stage in the history of Christianity. This crisis did not come about all at once. Spreading its roots back into the Enlightenment, it in fact indicates the breaking-up of a monocentrist approach, the dysfunctioning of the consensus given to a reservoir of discourse elaborated in order to counter heresies and reform movements and to maintain social cohesion as well as eternal survival.

Reacting to the Synod's plan for a universal catechism, Elias Zoghby has pointed out its political consequences: would not such a project risk taking us back to well before Vatican II, cutting short the researches undertaken by concerned bishops, by theologians, liturgists and canon lawyers, all trying to set the conclusions of the Council on their way to effective realisation?[8] There is nothing imaginary about such a risk. Effectively, even though it is designed to inspire and teach the baptised their faith, a catechism can only exist by 'fixing' the data of the deposit of faith in a particular form and structure. As a result, the official recipients of such a work can very easily be used as a pretext for 'really' reaching a different public: in this case, those bishops, theologians, liturgists and canon lawyers committed to and involved in the reform initiated by Vatican II. How could this be done? By insisting on basic principles that are established before making any deep analysis.

These considerations lead one to believe that, if the presentation of doctrine desired by the Synod Fathers takes the form of a compendium of truths drawn up on the basis of the four principles set out, this will amount to a decision to re-establish a certain order of things by trying to give an assured foundation to a particular structure of thought—and of society— which will 'shape the spirit of the Church for decades and perhaps centuries to come'.[9] So, in effect, dogmatists, liturgists, moralists and spiritual theologians would be put out to grass on a series of statements that in reality concern them more than those to whom they are officially addressed.

2. One general principle

The matter takes on another aspect if one envisages the hypothesis that the bishops' proposal is in fact appealing, not to four underlying principles, but to one overall principle governing presentation of doctrine, responding to a series of interrelated criteria. From a strategy for safeguarding the deposit of faith, we then move on to a strategy of proclamation, of promotion, integrated into a missionary purpose. Seen under this aspect, the proposal to produce a 'presentation of doctrine' made in a biblical 'and' liturgical manner, setting out an 'integral' doctrine and one 'at the same time' adapted to present-day Christian life, indicates the complexity and ambiguity of the pastoral-catechetical mission caught at the crossroads of a threefold reality. On one hand, it means identifying the biblical and liturgical resources of the Church, both enriched and wounded by the course of history. On the other, it means considering the responsibility of accompanying and guiding humankind along the 'new Way', despite the deep resistance shown by individuals and whole populations. Between the two, it would mean somehow accommodating recognition, verification and upholding of living forces, elements of genuine revelation taking shape here and now in these same individuals and populations.[10] The very principle of such a presentation is based on the sacramentality of life, taken as the space-time of proclamation and realisation of life converted to relationship with Jesus Christ. This is a principle which leaves space for the prophetic function, in the sense discussed by Norbert Greinacher in relation to practical theology.[11]

The principle of 'presentation of doctrine', such as can be deduced from the description of the life of the apostolic communities given in Acts (2:42–47; 4:32–35; 5:12–16), is always based on unifying experiences lived by those who chose the 'new Way': teaching, breaking bread, sharing goods, praying together. These elements stand out as criteria for recognition. They give an account of the way things worked, of polycentric (several but orientated toward one centre) 'ways' of growing (*augere*) in the 'new Way'. But what stands out is that this new way of living, based on conversion (*metanoia*) to Jesus Christ and following him, was opposed to many religious and cultural principles current in the context in which it was expressed. Theology, working here in close tandem with the life of these particular communities, is exercising its 'second step' critical function.

With regard to the aspect of producing a 'presentation of doctrine' adapted to the world today, it cannot be enough simply to set out a compendium of necessarily condensed texts—subject, in the final analysis, to the economics of printing requirements. Such a presentation would rather have to be conceived on the basis of a programme, in the sense in which the word is used in information technology. During the four centuries preceding Vatican II, the catechism became a school 'of words' guaranteeing cultural and religious identity in a cloistered world afraid of the world outside. The world of today has been transformed by information systems capable of providing, world-wide, data banks containing all the correct words in which to express religion. Catechesis can now more than ever become a school of 'the word' by developing a pedagogy that opens out deep spaces in human hearts and minds where the Spirit in person can join our spirit in witnessing that we are children of God (Rom. 8:16). The disciplines implied by the four criteria put forward by the Synod Fathers should intervene, together, as elements collaborating in the programme of such a school.

A biblical presentation of doctrine implies that the text of the Bible should be discovered as the account of a faith experience analogous to the—unwritten—experience of every believer and every present-day community. The history of the chosen people, told throughout the Bible, is, in essence, analogous to the route we all have to follow from the moment of conception to the final recognition, when what we now see as a dim reflection in a mirror we shall then see face to face (1 Cor. 13:12). From the standpoint of pastoral theology, the biblical dynamic, taken as an inspiration, stimulates, encourages and challenges, provides a support for the development of believers in their process of growing in faith. Catechetically presented, the Bible is an account offered to people, an account with an 'evocative' function—one, that is, capable of impressing itself on the deep experience of each person so as to bring out the full depth of meaning through the re-reading made by their precursors in faith. This evocation can, under the breath of the Holy Spirit, generate a word of faith not written down by today's believers, which can be transmitted on, making possible new accounts and new hearings which in turn, still under the inspiration of the Holy Spirit, produce new evocations.

'Liturgical' presentation of doctrine corresponds to a rich tradition in the Church. The liturgical field extends beyond the performance of rite to embrace the act and action of God revealed in the heart of humanity, the Word made flesh. Reforms undertaken since Vatican II have overturned a number of ingrained habits, ways of acting that were not lacking in influence on ways of being, though this influence was so subtle that it could never be encapsulated and was difficult to perceive or follow. Emilio Alberich devotes the final chapter of one of his books to an examination of the problem-ridden dialogue being undertaken today between liturgy and catechesis.[12] He brings out clearly the meaning and theoretical foundation of liturgy in relation to liturgical practices and activities. It is a fact that liturgical discourse has evolved considerably since Vatican II, but at the time there have never been so many 'impresarios' in the field, entirely devoted to dreaming up ways of staging celebrations without reference to the sacramentality of life, the 'more than meets the eye', the unsayable, the symbolic dimension, as Louis-Marie Chauvet calls it.[13] So would a catechism with a liturgical presentation have a liturgical 'basis' or show a liturgical 'way'? A liturgical 'way' implies care for living persons, welcoming them in their experience and, as Gérard Fourez says, awakening their lives in dimensions both already present and dormant.[14]

For this presentation of doctrine to 'present an integral teaching': here is a redundancy that can easily bring back memories of the tensions between orthodoxy and heterodoxy, between orthopraxis and heteropraxis. In this respect, Vorgrimler remarks that if the Synod's proposal means merely distinguishing between teaching put forward or very officially recognised by the magisterium, and hypotheses, interpretations and other legitimately offered essays in theological enlightenment, then the task would be as easy as it would be superfluous! If we are looking at a programme devoted to catechesis, we cannot rest content with a presentation of faith such as can be 'correctly formulated' to the ears of guardians of integral doctrine. What has to be put forward is an expression of faith that can be proclaimed and communicated to the whole human race. Surely this is the only way of imparting meaning to the final criterion: adaptation to the modern outlook on life? For surely this adaptation is itself a constantly dynamic process stemming from the responsibility of everyone for his or her mission? And it will always be on the level of reception—acceptance by the recipients—that, in the final analysis, the most objective evaluation of the changes effected, and therefore of the efficacity of the programme itself, will be made.

There will always be, at the outset of any presentation of doctrine that aims at a deep awakening of hearts, an overall process in which the different elements interact, with doctrine spreading its roots into the biblical narrative, which is itself inscribed in liturgical life, which both seeks and witnesses to the unceasing dialogues between God and God's creatures. Joseph Colomb said that bringing catechesis together with holy scripture, far from being an obstacle to doctrine, was in fact the only way of saving the concept, which had been compromised by a 'conceptualism' too ready to ignore 'facts'.[15]

Seeing the principle of presenting doctrine as a programme for the sake of its deeper inner reception by all is not, for that matter, at all foreign to the Synod Fathers' thinking. When, in points 5 and 6 of the Introduction to their 9 December document, they express their desire for 'a deeper reception of the Council', they speak of a process that has to go through four successive stages: wider and deeper knowledge of the Council, its inner assimilation, its reaffirmation in love, its passing into action in life. They add that interpretation of the Council's teaching should take account of each of the documents in themselves and in relation to one another: 'which would allow for a careful exposition of the integral meaning of the Council's proposals, which are often bound up with each other'. To attain this end, they propose that 'the local churches should work out a pastoral programme over the next few years, leading to new, wider and deeper knowledge and acceptance of the Council'. Should the principle underlying this presentation of conciliar teaching not inform the presentation of all Catholic doctrine, concerning both faith and morals?

Translated by Paul Burns

Notes

1. Two groups have done research into the production of catechisms: at the Theology Faculty of Laval University, Quebec, and the Higher Institute for Pastoral Catechetics at the Institut Catholique in Paris.

2. The work done by Jean-Claude Dhôtel and Elisabeth Germain is very enlightening on the origin and evolution of diocesan catechisms.

3. D. Maingueneau, *Sémantique de la polémique* (Lausanne 1983), p. 16.

4. C. Wackenheim, *La catéchèse, Que sais-je?* 2049 (Paris 1983), p. 7.

5. M. Angenot, 'Intertextualité, interdiscursivité, discours social', *Texte. Revue de critique et de théorie littéraire* 2 (1983), 108.

6. B. Plongeron, 'Premier bilan pour de nouvelles approches méthodologiques', *Une inconnue de l'histoire de la culture: La production des catéchismes en Amérique française*, ed. R. Brodeur and J.-P. Rouleau (Quebec 1986), pp. 445–446.

7. Course given at the Theology Faculty of Laval University, Quebec, Autumn 1988.

8. *Concilium* 188 (1986).

9. B. Marthaler, 'The Synod and the Catechism', *Concilium* 188 (1986).

10. Paul VI used similar terms in his Declaration *Nostra Aetate* of 28 October 1985 to describe the attitude of the baptised to the values proper to non-Christian religions.

11. N. Greinacher, 'La théologie pratique', unpublished, given at the Congress for Pastoral Studies at the University of Ottawa, June 1988.

12. *La catéchèse dans l'Eglise* (Paris 1986).

13. *Du symbolique au symbole. Essai sur les sacrements* (Paris 1979); *Symbole et sacrement. Une relecture sacramentelle de l'existence chrétienne* (Paris 1987).

14. *Les sacrements réveillent la vie. Célébrer les tensions et les joies de l'existence* (Paris 1982).

15. J. Colomb, *Aux sources du catéchisme. Histoire sainte et liturgie I* (Paris 1961), p. 11.

Jean Joncheray

What 'Catechism' for what 'World'?

THE EXPRESSION 'universal catechism', or in German 'Weltkatechismus' (world catechism) is calculated to set the imagination racing and to inflame contrary passions, either favourable or hostile to the project— whereas we do not necessarily know, so long as the project has not come to fruition, what this expression really conceals within itself.

This is because, in effect, where a work of this kind is concerned, the people for whom it is intended, the degree to which it is supposed to be normative, the purpose for which it is meant, are not secondary, accidental characteristics, but are an integral part of its very definition and affect its meaning. It is likely that once it has been drawn up and put into circulation, the book in question will not totally correspond either to the hopes or the fears, sometimes exaggerated, which it has aroused.

This article is not concerned to re-open the question of the interest or opportuneness of the project, of which the realisation is already far advanced, but some reflections on the notion which may be formed of a 'catechism' and also that of the 'world' or the 'universal', at this time when we are about to be presented with a catechism which is universal, or 'for the universal Church', may prove useful.

From these two aspects, the exhaustive treatment of these questions would necessitate lengthy analysis and the examination of points of view which are sometimes strongly contrasted. This article only presents a limited angle of attack and a point of view which may be debatable.

1. What catechism?

(a) A structure in dialogue form: from the redditio symboli *to questions-and-answers*

It will seem out-of-date, even provocative to some people, to make reference to the well-known system of questions and answers to evoke the kind of publication known as a catechism. It is true that the catechism properly so-called has not been restricted everywhere and from its origins to this type of presentation: 'The catechism may sometimes take the form of a continuous discourse', states the *Instruction pour bien faire le catéchisme et enseigner la doctrine chrétienne* published in Pont-à-Mousson in 1626.[1] The author is there referring to the sermon. But he much prefers the method which has become widely accepted: 'The method of catechising by questions and answers is the best.'[2] It is worth pausing to consider what is involved in this method (which there is obviously no question of proposing as a universal one!).

In the early Church, the candidate for admission to communion was made to recite the creed, either at the moment of baptism or when, on a journey, he arrived in a town in which he was unknown. In this latter case the statement of faith took on a quite remarkable degree of value as a means of recognition.

Within the rite of baptism, this moment of the *redditio symboli*: 'Do you believe in God the Father? Yes I believe in him . . .' was for a long time called, precisely, the catechesis. Of this primitive form of 'catechesis' represented by the *redditio symboli*, two aspects may be noted. The first is the symbolic function of the profession of faith as a sign of recognition and communion between believers in the God of Jesus Christ within the Church. It was also to fulfil this same purpose that the aspect of *regula fidei* of the creed operated, as a means of verification and control of the unity of the faith.

The second aspect which I wish to emphasise is that the progression towards the profession of faith is in a way enacted, in the rite of baptism, by the interplay of questions and answers. This leads one to think and to meditate on the fact that faith is a personal response, a personal commitment in answer to a call. In the liturgical rite, God's call is mediated through the minister of the Church who puts the question 'Do you believe?' Even if the rite strictly provides both the question and the answer, what is seen here is the candidate speaking for himself, what is being encouraged is the expression of the faith in the language and the culture of the newly baptised person. Moreover, one of the issues at stake in the drawing up of the Creed of Nicaea-Constantinople was to be the acknowledgment that it had become necessary to introduce into the *regula fidei* non-biblical terms and fourth-century language: *homoousios*.

It was therefore not by chance, in my opinion, that the first compilers of catechisms, both Protestant and Catholic, chose a dialogue form, and moreover a dialogue in which the roles are allocated in a precise way: the pastor questions and the disciple replies. It certainly seems, in fact, that it was deliberately chosen from among other well known forms of dialogue. Think of the dialogue in the course of the passover meal in Jewish families, where it is the child who asks the questions and the father who answers (*cf.* Exod. 12:26, Deut. 6:20); think of the *disputationes* in which thought progresses by refuting objections, as in the *Summa Theologica*, or of those 'scholastic colloquies', animated dialogues in which the protagonists are children or adolescents, pupils who converse on an equal level with their master,[3] which sixteenth-century humanist pedagogy used a great deal. The pedagogical choice predominant for two centuries in catechisms should therefore be related to the process of acceptance of the faith by the baptised person: it is the Church which asks: 'Do you believe?'

But this insistence on dialogue, this relationship established between God and the person who enters into the confession of the faith has frequently been forgotten over the years! This method has been, one might say, the victim of its own success, for it has spread far beyond the religious domain and one can 'make people recite lessons' in numerous spheres. The divergence has been discreet and it cannot always be easily perceived. One may note, for example, certain shades of difference in the designation of the participants in ancient writings: is it a question of the pastor and his disciple or of the teacher and his pupil? Or again, is it a matter of what one is invited to believe or of what it is necessary to know? Slight differences can already be seen between Luther's catechisms and those of Calvin. The emphasis may be put either on the call to a confession of faith or else on the logical structure of an organised and controlled system of knowledge.[4]

(b) Towards a complete, organic, universal exposition

The compiling of books containing organised questions and answers gradually introduced the logic of systematic exposition into the process of Christian initiation. That is to say that within the ecclesiological equilibrium to which the *redditio symboli* bore witness, it was the institutional aspect of the regulation of the faith which gained priority over the aspect of an invitation to the formulation of a personal response uniting with the faith of the Church. If the idea of dialogue is present at the beginning, the book, by presenting the answer at the same time as the question, no longer leaves any distance between the two. One thus runs the risk of crowding out the time needed for a personal response to mature, for the involvement of the person who says 'I believe' in a language which is truly his own. Thus one moves from the confession of faith, which supposes a personal involvement, to the objective exposition of the truths of the faith.

In the historical evolution of catechisms, the deviation is perceptible in a certain number of works. Sometimes the questions have become no more than pretexts, stylistic formulae, means of structuring a text which continues to unfold logically, developing the thought of the master. From the seventeenth to the nineteenth centuries in France, the most rationally logical schemes (what must be believed, what must be done, the means of doing it) were to gain ascendancy over those which referred back to a logical structure of entry into the mystery (preparation for the sacraments, the liturgical year . . .) or which were based on the theological virtues. One may wonder whether this evolution was a matter of chance or whether the production of catechisms was fatally drawn towards expositions of which the logic tended to present itself increasingly as a 'natural order' of exposition, which was to tend, just as logically, to present itself as universal. The ideal therefore came to be seen as the provision of just one single book for everyone.

But this could be at the cost of the personal progression involved in the approach to faith. And one understands why the movement of catechetical renewal in the twentieth century began with a rediscovery of the believer as subject.

It can only be a question here of a hypothesis, for one cannot generalise on the basis of a few observations drawn from the evolving history of the catechism. But it would involve a dangerous deviation for the faith if the meaning of the word *catechism* came to be reduced to a summary (or compendium) of the formulae which it is necessary to know, say and believe, and if the essence of the task of catechisation consisted of the universal imposition of these formulae. It can be easily understood that there could be a danger of producing the opposite effect to that which is supposedly being sought. This would in fact stifle personal expressions of faith and, as a result, those Christian communities which are genuinely rooted in diverse cultures. And one could also ask oneself whether there is not a relationship between this type of catechisation and the impoverishment of Christian thought and theology.

What matters is therefore the safeguarding of the ecclesiological equilibrium attested by the rite of baptism and by the creed as a symbol of the faith. It is a question of establishing a relationship between three elements: the Word of God expressed in the Church: scripture, tradition, magisterium, with its normative dimension; the personal identity of the believer, an identity which he shares with a human community, a culture in which he expresses his faith; and the encounter, both as confrontation and communion, with other present-day expressions of that same faith. It cannot merely be a matter of a simple juxtaposition. And one of the poles cannot be compensated for by another, as if it were enough to reaffirm the first when the others are deficient.

This interrelationship of elements presupposes flexibility if one wishes to prevent their jamming together. To seek to make them coincide in a pre-established synthesis is to close off the possibility of any vital circulation between them. By presenting answers even before the approach to the question has had time to be mapped out, by stating the norm before the individual expression has attempted to formulate itself through hesitant stammerings, one lowers too quickly the tension referred to, for example, by Cesare Bissoli, who wishes for 'an instrument of which the objective normativity does not destroy the space available for a personal journey towards faith and therefore for its personal reformulation.'[5] Certainly, a tension does exist in fact. To imagine that the totality of individual expressions of faith could reconstitute, as if by magic, an ecclesial creed which had never been set out beforehand is as unrealistic as to believe that it would be sufficient to impose a text in a particular language, and thus in a particular culture, for everyone thereafter to have to do no more than translate it, and that every source of ambiguity would thereby be removed. It is a question, in fact, of working towards the integration, never fully achieved, of all the 'I's into an ecclesial 'we'.

How, therefore, might a universal catechism contribute to a better ecclesiological equilibrium? It would first be necessary to know whether, in the text of the Synod of 1985, which speaks of a 'catechism *or* global exposition of the whole of Catholic doctrine (compendium)', *catechism* and *compendium* are considered as synonymous or whether a choice, an alternative, is involved. The term *catechism* can refer to different things, according to the cultural areas and countries in which differing practices may have existed. In France we have witnessed a diminution of the meaning of the term *catechism* to an unalterable *summary* which must be learned by heart (and this is also what is suggested by the word compendium), so much so that it has been judged necessary to change the word *catechism* to indicate that what was desired was the rediscovery of all the richness of the catechetical process.

In Italy, Cesare Bissoli seems to be able to distinguish between catechism and compendium and on the basis of the latter word, used by the Synod, he argues that 'it cannot be a question of a catechism which is unitary or unique and universal, already put together and ready for use' and insists on the contrary on its 'reference point' aspect which is in fact referred to in the subsequent passage in the Synodical text.[6]

Whatever the truth of the matter, it seems certain that for such a work to be able to exercise a symbolic function it is important that it should be situated, like all normative texts, at a healthy distance from everyday local practice. Otherwise it would be in danger of artificially blocking the process of integration which must bring the various elements together, and of cutting short the flowering of living expressions of the faith and of a whole variety of means of guiding people towards it. But if the balance between the 'I's and the 'we' is never completely achieved, if the Church is an organism in the process of growing 'until we all reach together the state of maturity, the stature of Christ in its fullness' (Eph. 4:13), then it may be foreseen that until that state is attained numerous remodellings and variations will constantly be needed.

2. What kind of universality for the catechesis?

In the era of satellite television and increasingly rapid travel, one frequently hears it said that our planet has become a global village. One must admit, however, that a minimum of observation is enough to make us realise that mankind is still far from resolving all the problems resulting from the building of the Tower of Babel.

No doubt the proposal of a universal catechism is underpinned in some minds by the idea that we have now reached a certain level of universal common culture, of planetary unity, a new *koinē* on which the *koinonia*, the community of the faithful, might be constructed.

This may explain the parallels which have been suggested with the Council of Trent. In this connection, Gilbert Adler reminds us: 'The success of the Roman catechism and of the theology conveyed by it is due, in large measure, to the cultural unity which sustains it.'[7] But I think, like him, that we are no longer in the same circumstances and that our situation is not one of cultural unity. Unless one considers the problem of inculturation no longer relevant.

I shall not deal directly here with the question of inculturation and of the contribution which a single reference work may make to it, since several articles in this issue of *Concilium* are directly devoted to this subject. I shall approach from another angle the question of the idea of the universal which is presupposed by the project of a universal catechism. And this will in fact bring me back once more to the question 'What catechesis?' rather than the question 'What world?'

I observe in fact that catechetical activity is not envisaged in the same way everywhere, but varies according to the different situations of the Church in the countries concerned. As a result, I ask myself the question: Does not the provision of a universal catechism presuppose an ecclesiastical and therefore catechetical situation which is more or less the same from one country to another?

(a) To whom is catechesis directed?

There exists a traditional terminology, recalled for example by Emilio Alberich: 'In the normal, and most classical, tradition, *three great moments, three functions*, are distinguished in the service of the Word: *evangelisation* (or *kerygma*, missionary preaching), *catechesis* and *liturgical preaching* (or homily, preaching to the community).'[8] But he points out that vocabulary evolves: the word *evangelisation*, in particular, has taken on a fullness of meaning which it previously lacked, notably since Paul VI's apostolic exhoration *Evangelii nuntiandi*.

To take one example, let us note how the Spanish bishops, in their pastoral directions for catechesis in present-day Spain,[9] make use of these terms in order to adapt them to their country's situation:

> Within the dynamic process of evangelisation, *missionary activity* directed towards non-believers should not be confused with *pastoral activity* directed towards believers. In this sense the distinction established by *Catechesi tradendae* between pastoral and missionary activities serves only to corroborate the affirmation of the Council: 'Missionary activity directed towards non-believers *differs* from the pastoral activity which must be developed with the faithful' (*Ad gentes* 6).
>
> Catechesis is situated, precisely, between these two *phases* of evangelisation: it follows missionary activity and prepares the foundations of the Christian community so that the pastoral activity which must take place within it may fully bear fruit.[10]

Thus the classical distinction is here made again, but producing an unstable or transitory situation with regard to catechesis. Are its recipients covered at the same time by both missionary and pastoral activity? or not really by either? Catechesis would seem, therefore, to relate most closely to 'catechumenal activity (with the newly converted)'.[11]

But the Spanish bishops do not stop short at this point, and, observing their country's situation, ask themselves the question: 'Do not the majority of our Christian people need a missionary proclamation of the Gospel, before catechesis in the proper sense of the term?'[12] They answer this question in the affirmative. And this leads them to propose, for the expression 'missionary catechesis', the following definition:

> Catechesis which is directed towards those baptised Christians who, although linked to the Church through a certain level of religious practice, need an initial conversion. It is distinct from *catechesis in its proper sense*, which presupposes conversion, and also from the *initial proclamation*, in the strict sense, which is directed to those who feel detached from the Church or have lost their faith.[13]

It can be clearly seen at this point that the traditional categories are insufficient to contain a complex local reality and that, moreover, the terms will have different meanings according to whether Spain is considered as a part of Christendom or of the 'mission field',[14] or, yet again, whether one considers that both of these expressions are inadequate to describe the situation.

The question, it seems to me, therefore remains essentially unanswered: For whom is catechesis intended? It includes two aspects. The first is theological. Everything depends therefore on the breadth of significance to be given to the term, whether by distinguishing it from the terms evangelisation, *kerygma*, liturgical preaching, etc ... and making the catechetical period a transitory stage in a person's life, like a catechumenate or a neophytate; whether, on the contrary, by making catechetical activity a dimension of the total activity of the Church, so that catechesis for adults may be seen as lasting throughout their Christian life. It is thus, for example, that John Paul II defines it at the beginning of *Catechesi tradendae*: 'the totality of efforts undertaken within the Church to make disciples, to aid men to believe that Jesus is the Son of God so that by faith they may have life in his name, to educate and instruct them in this life and so build up the Body of Christ.'[15] He later clarifies this definition and lays great stress on the diversity of those who undergo catechesis in the fifth part, which has the very clear title: 'All men need to be catechised'.

The second aspect depends on a vision of the world, or, more exactly, of the Church in the world: does the distinction between the mission field and countries which are already evangelised, seen in the decree *Ad gentes*, still correspond to reality? And if so, what about those countries in which a second evangelisation is thought to be necessary? is this second evangelisation a catechetical activity?

It therefore seems to me necessary to ask oneself whether the idea of a universal catechism presupposes a homogeneous situation, both for individuals and peoples, with respect to the Gospel message, or whether on the contrary it is capable of taking account of the existence of Catholics, non-Catholic Christians, various kinds of believers, non-believers, and also baptised persons who are far from the Church, people whose religious situation is changeable and at present ill-defined, etc . . . Certain catechisms (including the one which I learned as a child) used to begin with the question: 'What is your religion? I belong to the Catholic religion.' Many of today's intended recipients would, rightly or wrongly, close the book before the second question.

(b) Into what activities is catechesis integrated?

The question of the intended recipients of catechesis leads on to the importance attached to catechesis on its own, whereas it can only be understood when incorporated into an ecclesiastical totality which is by no means to be found everywhere. What is involved here is the idea one has of the transmission of culture, of the modalities of belonging to a group, of personal and collective adhesion to certain values or ways of life. It seems useful to situate the demand for catechesis among the present-day demands made on the Church in a world which does not always know where it may find its ethical reference-points or a basis for living together in a social consensus, or quite simply a common life. Catechists can only make their contribution, but are they not being asked to take on alone a burden which they are only capable of bearing in collaboration with others?

A phrase of Emilio Alberich, assessing the good and bad points of catechesis in Europe, notes an observation which is widely shared: 'The catechesis traditionally included in the organism of Christian initiation, now very often finds itself deprived of this organic context, exposed to contradictory tensions and demands and weighted down by an excessive burden: responsibility for a process of education in the faith which, in fact, it must bear all alone.' And he refers a few lines later to 'one of the most serious and difficult problems of contemporary European pastoral theology: the need to re-examine in depth the whole process of Christian initiation'.[16]

Putting forward a catechism can therefore only be understood as one element of the Church's total activity. Unless one imagines, as it was sometimes thought in the century following the Council of Trent, which witnessed the first massive dissemination of popular literature, that to combat religious ignorance is almost infallibly to reform morals. Richelieu said at the beginning of his *Instruction du chrétien*, speaking of the way of salvation: 'When it is impossible for you not to know it, it will be easy for you to follow it . . .'[17]

But, on a wider scale, to seek to offer a contribution by the Church, in a world which is seeking points of reference, consensus, reasons for living, yet which, however, does not see itself on a global scale as living under the authority of the legitimate Pastors of the Church, to seek to be for this world a sign and a call, would mean entering into a conversation, a debate, a dialogue with this world. At the end of our exploration, we discover many questions and answers. It now remains for us to write them together.

Translated by L. H. Ginn

Notes

1. *Instruction pour bien faire le catéchisme et enseigner la doctrine chrétienne* (Pont-à-Mousson 1626), p. 344.
2. *Idem.*, p. 342.
3. *Cf.* Jean-Claude Margolin's contribution at the colloquium of 11–12 March 1988, at the Institut Catholique, Paris: *Aus origines du catéchisme paroissial et des manuels diocésains de catéchisme en France, 1500–1600* (in course of publication).
4. Jacques Audinet's contribution at the above colloquium.
5. Cesare Bissoli 'Un catechismo per il nostro tempo? Attualità e senso del dibattito sulla attuale proposta di un "catechismo per la chiesa universale"', *Il catechismo ieri e oggi* (Turin 1987), p. 75.
6. *Art. cit.*, p. 82.
7. Gilbert Adler, 'Vers un catéchisme universel: fantasmes et réalités', *Etudes* (juillet-août 1987), 99.
8. Emilio Alberich, *La catéchèse dans l'Eglise* (Paris 1986), p. 57; (*Catechesi e prassi ecclesiale* (Turin 1982), p. 44).
9. Comision episcopal de Enseñanza y catequesis, *La catequesis de la communidad* (Madrid 1983).
10. *Op. cit.*, pp. 19–20.
11. *Op. cit.*, p. 17.
12. *Op. cit.*, p. 25, *cf. Catechesi tradendae* 19.
13. *Op. cit.*, p. 173.
14. J. Lopez, *España, país de mision* (Madrid 1979).
15. *Catechesi tradendae* 1. The whole thesis expounded in this text is very enlightening on this question.
16. Emilio Alberich, 'Regard sur la catéchèse européenne', *Catéchèse* (juillet-octobre 1985), no. 100–101, 169.
17. Richelieu, Bishop of Luçon, *Instruction du chrétien* (Paris 1618).

David Tracy

World Church or World Catechism: The Problem of Eurocentrism

1. World and worlds

THE HOPE for an adequate 'world catechism' seems, at best, illusory. At least this will remain the case until such time as further reflection is afforded both the terms 'catechism' and the term 'world'. As a genre, 'world catechism' seems to imply too great a common mind and common language on *how* to articulate the heart of the faith cross-culturally. A 'world catechism' seems to call into question the reality of necessary enculturation in a pluralistic world. Catechisms, after all, are, as a genre, even more complex than their closest analogue, a 'short confession' of the common faith. Any ecclesial confession, is, of course, as deeply culturally embedded as all other realities. Nevertheless, short confessions of the faith are theologically, and culturally, through their relative modesty of aim, often able to transcend their cultural embeddedness to bespeak the central realities of the faith to readers and hearers from cultures other than the culture of origin. The strictly confessional aspects of the great catechisms are—by their fidelity to the common faith of the Church—also available to all informed readers.

But, strictly as a genre, a 'world catechism' involves more than the common confession of the common faith: it also entails an assumption that the human situation to which the great doctrines and symbols of the common confession speak is so clear and stable that it is, by definition, cross-cultural and trans-historical (hence 'world'). Yet this assumption seems highly doubtful both culturally and historically. In a situation where even transcendental philosophies of communication (Apel, Habermas) are both more modest in their transcendental (or 'quasi-transcendental') claims and far more attendant than their 'philosophy of consciousness' predecessors to the linguistic and therefore the social-economic-cultural-historical embeddedness of all transcendental formulations, it is odd to find theologians untroubled by the possibility of a *world* catechism.

These philosophical difficulties, moreover, pale besides the actual theological realities. At the very moment when there are persuasive reasons to believe (Rahner, Bulhmann) that the Church is ceasing to be a Eurocentric church and becoming rather a global, polycentric church, a plea for a 'world catechism' seems curiously short-sighted. Consider that other great watershed period of church history, the period that produced the New Testament as the Church's book. There one witnesses the shift from a Jewish Christianity to both a Jewish and many forms of Gentile Christianity. Does not early Christianity show how many situationally embedded confessions and catechetical instructions were necessary to maintain the common confession in Jesus the Christ in so many different cultural situations? The situations of the communities of Mark, Matthew, Luke, John, Paul, James, the pastoral epistles, the Book of Revelation are sufficiently distinct to demand often very different renderings of the common narrative, the common following of Christ, the common confession of Christ in different—often very different—cultural and historical situations of the first century of Christianity.

Indeed that early New Testament period is the surest analogue to our own situation. Catholic Christianity can no longer afford to be Eurocentric anymore than early Christianity could afford to be purely Judaic if it would reach all the Gentiles in ways that they could understand and appropriate the common faith in their own cultural forms. Analogously, the different situations in contemporary Europe itself—West, Central, and East; the different situations in the North-South split across the world; the different situations in Latin America, North America, Africa, Asia, and throughout the now polycentric Catholic world shows that (as in the New Testament period itself) the hope for fidelity to the common confession of all Catholics demands—ethically, religiously, and theologically—the closest attention to and honouring of the different economic, social cultural and historical situations of the different Catholic peoples.

Every classic in any culture is highly particular in origin and expression yet universal in effect. Such, in essence, is the paradox of the classic as distinct from the period-piece. The always-available timeliness of every classic text, image, ritual. action, person (*e.g.*, saints), symbol comes from and only from the willingness to undertake the journey of intensification into one's own particular experience, culture, tradition. Only in that manner does any classical expression in any culture emerge. The classic expressions of the Catholic tradition render a sense for the concrete as *particular*, *local*,—the really concrete—into a natural sense. Catholics know, almost as a second instinct, that one reaches the concrete whole—the 'universal'— only in and through the journey into one's own particularity—this family, this people, this locality, this local church, community, folk, heritage.

A recognition of the all pervasive reality of grace, of the need to focus upon every particular manifestation in the light of the paradigmatic self-manifestation-incarnation of God in Jesus Christ is the religious and theological vision that forms something like a 'second sense' in Catholics for appreciating the local, the concrete, the particular. That 'second sense' is what must be encouraged in every local church as it is in the Church universal: God and God's grace are here in this particular community. That particularity must be honoured. It is true that the paradigmatic which is the real is none other than the event of God, Jesus Christ. And what that extraordinary, paradigmatic event also reveals is the extraordinariness of the ordinary—of the local, the concrete, the particular as our proximate clue here and now to the whole. To miss that clue is to risk missing the paradigmatic reality present to and in it. It is to miss the fact that the all (God-self-world) are best understood in and through the particular. For if God is love, if all is graced, then the surest route to that love and to that universality is here, now, in the really concrete, the 'each', the local and the particular joined to the universal.

In sum, the concept 'world' in proposals for a 'world catechism' seems as unexamined as the difference between the genres of a 'short confession of the faith' and an always situationally oriented 'catechism'. At this time in history the other 'transcendental' discipline, philosophy, now acknowledges its Western character and its need to pay close attention to language and thereby cultural and historical differences if it is to be faithful in our context to its own transcendental aim. It is, then, puzzling to find theology—at least the theology informing proposals for a 'world catechism'—so insensitive to the need for historical contextualisation and cultural enculturation for all catechetical (and thereby situational) renderings of the common confession of the faith. There is a need for more attention to the Eurocentric notion of 'world' in any proposals for a world catechism.

In one sense, 'Europe' is not a geographical expression. Rather (as in Troeltsch and Rendtorff) the expression 'Europeanism' has a culture-transcending reality: not only in the global use of Western science but also in such ethical-political and culturally transcending realities as 'human rights'. The ability of European culture (or any great culture) to be self-transcending is not in question here. What is in question is the assumption that European (including North American) ways of thought are, without careful argument on each specific claim (*e.g.*, human rights), by definition (*i.e.*, by European definition) sufficiently culturally transcending to constitute the 'world'. This *hubris*, with its clear suggestion of cultural colonialism, is what unthinking Western scientists and philosophers can sometimes still indulge in. But that Christian theologians should thus concur is deeply troubling. For, *pace* Hilaire Belloc, it is not true that 'Europe is the faith; and the faith is Europe'. Rather Christianity is clearly now in fact a world-church. And any refusal to acknowledge that reality theologically—even under the good intentions of a 'world catechism' whose Eurocentric character is clear—should be resisted theologically. All the great symbols and doctrines of the common faith are culturally transcending. But, in a paradox which philosophically can be expressed as the paradox of the manifestation of truth as a 'concrete universal'—this universality must always be enculturated in each particular culture in accordance with its particularity. Catholicism, at its best, has always acknowledged this: as in the relative affirmation of some so-called 'pagan' elements as *preparatio evangelii* and not, therefore, to be simply destroyed but transformed. At this moment in its extraordinary history, Catholic Christianity is most faithful to its very catholicity by affirming the common confession of faith in many (not only European) cultural forms. This need and this promise can be seen in recent theological and ecclesial developments of every one of the great symbols and doctrines of the faith. As a single example, consider how the central doctrine of salvation has been and continues to be both culturally and historically embedded and only thereby culturally and historically transcending.

2. Christian salvation: its basic elements and its need for contextualisation

1. The Christian understanding of salvation begins with an experimental claim. That claim is this: A Christian in whatever culture experiences a state of some releasement from some experienced bondage, and in that very release, the Christian experiences a sense that this healing is from God. However fragmentary such experiences may be, such experiences are experienced by Christians as real and as salvific. The experience is inevitably dialectical. The experience is, first, an experience of release from some powerful bondage. Consider, in history and different cultures, how the experience of salvation is distinctly construed: a release from guilt by the forgiveness of sin, a release from the bondage of an anxious sense of radical transience, from anxiety in the face of death, from anxiety in the face of

the seeming meaninglessness or absurdity of existence, and from the bondage of a sense of being trapped without hope of release in systemically distorted structures of one's individual psyche or the massive global suffering caused by oppression in society and history. The experience of salvation is, at the same time, an experience of release *to* some new way of existing as an authentic human being: an experience of freedom for living in the world without ultimate mistrust of existence; a freedom for accepting the created world and one's own finitude as essentially good; the freedom for accepting the fact of our own acceptance by God despite sin and guilt; the freedom for facing death as not the final world; the freedom for acting for others with the trust that such actions ultimately do make a difference; the freedom for accepting experiences of peace, joy, and understanding as manifestations, however fragmentary, of the presence of ultimate reality itself; the freedom for joining the struggle for economic and political justice.

2. All such experiences, like *all* experiences, bear interpretative elements. Even aside from the presently unnecessary complexities of hermeneutic theory, this means that: (a) there is no experience without some understanding; and (b) every act of understanding is itself an act of interpretation.

In the Christian case, the interpretative elements in these experiences of releasement and wholeness are many and always historically and culturally embedded. For such experiences are named not only 'releasement' but 'salvation'. This means that a Christian experiences—understands—these salvific experiences as gift and task from God. More precisely, these experiences are Christian experience of *faith in* the God who in Jesus Christ disclosed what ultimate reality is (*viz.*, the holy mystery of embracing and encompassing love). These experiences disclose as well to the Christian who we are and who we can become (*viz.*, finite but estranged human beings who can be released from bondage by faith in Jesus Christ and thereby be able to follow the way of radical love of God and neighbour).

3. The experience of 'releasement-wholeness' as an experience of Christian salvation is, therefore, Christianly construed as an experience of response to the God disclosed in Jesus Christ. This is, in Christian terms, an experience of faith. Faith entails, but does not first *mean*, faith as a *belief that* certain cognitive meanings are true. Christian faith, as an experience of salvation, fundamentally means a *belief in* (a trust in, acceptance of) the God of Jesus Christ. Faith is the following of Christ. From that interpretative experience of releasement and wholeness as an experience of radical trust in and loyalty to the God decisively manifested in Jesus Christ, all else flows: the recognition that this experience is gift,

grace and task; the recognition that the saving initiative in the experience is God's, as the decisive manifestation of that God who is love; the recognition that this experience of being released from whatever compulsive bondage once trapped us is also a release to a new way of life—a way of faith working through love and justice, a way attempting to follow Christ as that way is disclosed in the ministry, teaching, death, and resurrection of that Jesus who is the Christ *i.e.*, the one who is present in individual and communal Christian experience and decisively manifests the nature of ultimate reality as the God who is love. Faith is praxis and praxis is always embedded in a particular culture.

4. The fundamental Christian witness to salvation is a witness which is grounded in those primary interpretative experiences of 'salvation' as release from bondage and release to the new way of Jesus Christ. As interpretative the experience is also particular. In this salvific experiential context, therefore, the fundamental Christian confession remains 'I (we) believe *in* Jesus Christ *with* the apostles'. This confession does not read, note, 'I believe in the historical Jesus', nor 'I belive in Christ', nor, 'I believe *in* the apostles'.

The confession means what it says: 'I (we) believe *in* Jesus Christ *with* the apostles'. To observe the force of the preposition 'in' is to note the grounding of Christian salvific experience (both individually and communally) in the reality of God's disclosure in Jesus Christ. To add the phrase '*with* the apostles' is to recall the need for further theological criteria for interpreting what we mean by 'the apostles'. This is also to recall how, in a historically and hermeneutically conscious age, we late twentieth-century Christians in whatever culture can interpret ourselves as in continuity with those first witnesses to Christ.

On this reading, therefore, any modern Christian soteriology must attempt ever new formulations attentive to a particular culture's needs on which 'Christian salvation' is (as above). Those formulations will prove, at best, relatively adequate interpretations of (a) the fundamental questions in our present situation (the search for salvation from bondage and for a new way of authentic freedom); (b) the categories best fitted to articulate this salvific experience of Jesus Christ as the decisive manifestation of God as encompassing Love; (c) categories which attempt fundamental but critical continuity with 'the apostles' as the original witnesses to that salvific experience. In fact, this process of continuous interpretation of Christian salvation has occurred, is occurring, and, as long as Christians experience salvation at all, will continue to occur in ever-new situations and cultures.

These seem to be the basic constants of the Christian understanding of salvation. In our own day, renewed interest has arisen in one further question: granted these cross-cultural constants in the Christian confession of salvation, should we also say that Chritian 'salvation' is today the empowering gift and command for Christians to enter wholeheartedly into the struggle for political and social liberation? Is salvation properly construed as a total liberation which demands political action? This lies at the heart of much contemporary Christian debate on salvation today. It is a central example of the need for enculturation—even of so central a symbol for the Christian as salvation.

3. The liberating example of liberation theologies in a polycentric Church

In one sense it is obvious that Christian salvation can be described through the metaphor 'liberation'. For both the Jewish and the Christian understandings of salvation, liberation by God from bondage has been a central biblical and post-biblical metaphor: classically in Exodus and in the prophetic trajectories. Moreover, 'bondage', the correlate metaphor to liberation, is frequently used to describe what we are saved or liberated *from*. Indeed, 'bondage' as suggested above is a constant basic element through all the shifts of metaphor for the more positive salvific experience (salvation *for* or *to*) in the history of Christian reflection. More exactly, death, suffering and guilt-sin are frequently described in terms of 'bondage' which only divine liberation-salvation can liberate or save us from. In this classical Christian perspective, there is (or should be) little controversy on the appropriateness of describing salvation as total liberation: from guilt-sin, from death and transience, and, in principle, from any bondage which entraps us.

What the classical Christian interpretations of salvation and post-modern Western readings of our situation share is a belief in the existence of systemic distortions (illusions) and not mere errors. Indeed, illusion is our real problem. Where Christian construals differ from post-modern secular accounts is also clear: Christian understandings of 'sin' can (and should) include a recognition of such systemic distortions as sexism, racism, classism, anti-Semitism, elitism. And yet the Christian understanding of 'sin' is not exhausted by these accounts—above all, since sin is primordially interpreted as sin against Ultimate Reality or God. Just as importantly, Christian understandings of salvation can (and again should) include a recognition of the need for joining wholeheartedly in the modern and post-modern journeys of political, cultural, social emancipation and freedom. Yet again, Christian salvation, as grounded in God as origin and goal of all human action, cannot be exhausted by any account which claims that our emancipation can be achieved through the sole use of some new emancipatory method of struggle.

This suggests that Metz is correct to insist that 'emancipation' and 'redemption' (in his terms) are not synonymous but must be dialectially related in any Christian understanding of redemption-salvation. This also suggests that the liberation theologians and the feminist theologians are correct to insist that the often forgotten, perhaps even repressed, biblical metaphor 'liberation' is a good metaphor (and when joined to the other critical theoretical resources, a good concept) to describe Christian salvation in our context. More exactly, as soon as any Christian theologian understands 'freedom from' and 'freedom for' as crucial categories for understanding Christian salvation, she/he must also account for the histories of freedom and the linked histories of suffering exposed by all modern Western and non-Western accounts of our systemic distortions.

There is also no need to deny the primordial Christian character of 'freedom from' as freedom from guilt-sin. Nor is there any need to deny, on inner Christian grounds, the 'freedom from' death in Christian salvation—as those histories of suffering of oppressed peoples which always accompany the histories of freedom (of the 'victors') suggest in new and forceful ways. And yet, there is no need to retreat into a hardened individualism or a weak personalism. Indeed there is every good reason for Christian theologians aware of the pervasive reality of social and political structures in all our exercises of freedom, and the actuality of unconscious psychic and linguistic structures in all our exercises of emancipatory reason, to abandon all purely individualist and personalist accounts of salvation.

In sum, Christian salvation is appropriately described as insisting upon total liberation of the individual *and* of all those linguistic, psychic, social, and political structures which form individuals whether they will it or not. The fragmentary signs of such liberation may, therefore, be found not only in the salvific experiences of healed individuals but in the struggles for political and social liberation of oppressed peoples. There is no individual freed from these structures (oppressed and alienated oppressors alike). It is not adequate to speak of Christian liberation-salvation of any individual while ignoring those structures of bondage which inflict themselves upon each and all. For example, there is truth in Gustavo Gutiérrez's charge to European and North American theologians that 'your history of freedom is not ours'—as in his insistence that 'our' notions of 'development' do not fit the Latin American situation which demands social and political liberation, including liberation from 'our' accounts of what counts as 'development'.

A similar analysis of any of the other classic symbols and doctrines (*e.g.*, 'creation' in African Christianity; the 'self' in Asian Christianity) of the common Christian confession could easily yield the same conclusion as this analysis of salvation: there are theological commonalities that transcend history and culture but these commonalities always have been and always must be embedded in particular histories and cultures. It is unlikely, at best, that any 'world catechism' can succeed in fidelity to all the different contextualisations of the common confession of faith of a global church. It is all too unlikely that such a catechism will prove another example of an unwelcome and unacknowledged Eurocentrism in a polycentric world church. Like the New Testament Church, the present Church has the opportunity— indeed the *kairos*—to leave behind its former cultural and historical Eurocentric view of the 'world' and meet the world as it is in all its diversity, challenge, and promise. Good pastoral praxis, as the New Testament Church knew, is good theology. Good theology is culturally and historically transcending only by its fidelity to its own particularity. Good catechisms are good by their fidelity to the same paradox of transcendence through the common confession rendered in distinct ways for distinct cultures. No one needs to become European to join the 'world'. No one should be expected to become European to join their narrative, their culture, their particularity to Jesus Christ and his culture-transcending Church.

Bibliography

1 On the transcendental and transcultural:
   (1) Jürgen Habermas, *Theorie des Kommunikativen Handelns* I & II, (Frankfurt am Main 1980–1981).
   (2) Trutz Rendtorff, ed. *Europäsche Theologie, Versuche einer Ortbestimmung* (Gütersloh 1980).
   (3) David Tracy, *Plurality and Ambiguity: Hermereutics, Religion, Hope* (San Franscisco 1987/London 1988).

2 On salvation in a world church:
   (1) Edward Schillebeeckx, *On Christian Faith: The Spiritual, Ethical and Political Dimensions* (New York 1987).
   (2) Wayne A. Meeks, *The First Urban Christians: The Social World of the Apostle Paul* (New Haven, Conn. 1983).
   (3) Rosemary Radford Ruether, *To Change the World: Christology and Cultural Criticism* (New York 1981).
   (4) Anne E. Carr, *Transforming Grace: Christian Tradition and Women's Experience* (San Francisco 1988).
   (5) Gustavo Gutiérrez, *The Power of the Poor in History* (New York 1979/London 1984).
   (6) Roger Haight, *An Alternative Vision: An Interpretation of Liberation Theology* (New York 1985).

(7) Johann-Baptist Metz, *Faith in History and Society* (New York/London 1980).

(8) Schubert M. Ogden, *Faith and Freedom: Toward a Theology of Liberation* Nashville, Tn. 1979).

PART II

Examples of Ecclesial and Theological Experiences

Berard Marthaler

The Catechism Genre, Past and Present

THE CATECHISM is as plastic as potter's clay. From the time that catechisms first became popular in the sixteenth century, the genre included a variety of works of different lengths and style. Martin Luther and Peter Canisius edited small catechisms for the use of children and the uneducated as well as large compendia of Christian doctrine for use by pastors, teachers and the educated. The Heidelberg Catechism (1564) and the Catechism of the Council of Trent (1565) were confessional documents in that they presented the 'official' teaching of the Reformed and Catholic traditions respectively. The former used a question-and-answer format; the latter, organised into four parts (Creed, Sacraments, the Commandments, and Prayer), used a discursive style. The short catechism in the Anglican Book of Common Prayer, also in question-and-answer form, was integral to the liturgy of the confirmation rite.

In the Roman Catholic tradition the history of the catechism is complex. Most works of this genre that appeared between 1550 and 1650 were compiled by individuals, or by religious orders and communities of priests. The Catechism of the Council of Trent was unique. It is the only catechism that was commissioned by a general council and, issued under papal authority, given official status for the entire Church. The Tridentine Catechism was not intended for common use, but as a source book to aid the clergy in instructing the people. The preface included some general principles about teaching, and in the seventeenth century many editions included an appendix that suggested catechetical themes to be developed in connection with the Sunday readings.

From the beginning catechisms were intended to serve both as pedagogical tools and confessional documents. It is this dual purpose that has given these manuals an importance beyond their intrinsic value, and has caused them to be judged by conflicting criteria and priorities. The priority of catechists and teachers is the effective communication of the Christian message according to the background and capacity of the learner. Ecclesiastical authorities and theologians tend to judge catechisms in terms of orthodoxy and completeness. In subtle ways, catechisms have also served an apologetic purpose. Few were openly argumentative or polemical, but most were shaped by the controversies of the time. Issues that divide the churches are given more attention than the faith they hold in common.

1. An early critique of catechisms

In what is probably the earliest critical examination of the purpose, contents and method of catechisms, the great church historian Claude Fleury (1640–1723) describes the dilemma faced by all authors of catechisms. Are their works to be judged as theological treatises or as effective pedagogical tools?

In the manner of the times, the long title of Fleury's work clearly described its contents: *An Historical Catechism, containing a Summary of the Sacred History and Christian Doctrine.*[1] The introduction, based on Fleury's experience as a tutor and his familiarity with the ancient sources, provided a brief overview of the history of catechetical practices. The earliest form of catechesis was the narrative—the telling of the story of God's creation, the promulgation of the Covenant: first with the Israelites and later the New Covenant with the disciples of Jesus. Fleury cites the example of St Stephen whose discourse was a recital of facts, reminding his listeners of all that God had done for them. Similarly, the Church Fathers grounded their instruction on the story of God's intervention into human history from the beginning of the world to the proclamation of the Gospel message. *Narratio* was basic to the method that St Augustine bequeathed to the Christian West. It endured as the chief form of catechesis, according to Fleury, as long as the Church maintained the ancient discipline of the catechumenate, that is, until the ninth century.

As infant baptism more and more became the common practice, the creed, itself an example of *narratio*, became the focal point of catechesis. Children memorised the words that were then explained to them in homilies and public instructions. In the medieval period the forms were kept but they degenerated into formalities. 'The misery of the times', the development of vernacular tongues, and the ignorance of the clergy conspired to bring about a neglect of even rudimentary catechesis. From the tenth century on, councils and synods found it necessary to mandate that bishops and priests teach the people, at least, the Creed and the Lord's Prayer. Catechesis was reduced to memorising a few formulas with little attention to the story of creation and salvation or knowledge of the scriptures.

Writing sometime about 1683, Fleury allowed that ignorance remained but he also noted great improvement over the situation of two hundred years earlier. He attributed 'the most wonderful fruits' (p. 36) to the catechism and the efforts of St Ignatius of Loyola and his disciples to catechise children. Although Fleury recognised the value of catechisms, he was critical of many then in use. They were generally the work of theologians who filled the text with scholastic distinctions and knew little of the ways of children. Catechisms written specifically for children and the uneducated lost their focus because they had abandoned the *narratio*. They mingled 'facts', that is, random biblical stories and lives of the saints, with doctrine and theological opinion. The trinitarian and narrative structure of the Creed never emerged from the doctrinal formulas and theological explanations.

Fleury's criticisms of the catechisms of the time provided a justification for his own work. He granted that individuals who are ignorant of the Christian story, may know the minimum truths that are absolutely necessary for salvation, but he argued that the purpose of catechesis is to render Christians capable of taking an active part in the life of the Christian community and profiting from it. Catechesis ought, at the very least, to prepare people to understand the liturgy of the word and to participate in the celebration of the sacred mysteries. The catechism should be a means to that end; mastery of the catechism is not an end in itself. Knowledge of doctrine is not a measure of faith.

The best method of teaching, Fleury said, is not that which appears most natural to theologians and scholars who consider truths abstractly and only in relationship to other truths. A catechism must be judged by other criteria than orthodoxy and completeness. To be effective catechisms must present the truths of religion and the principles of morality in a way that carries them into the minds and hearts of the hearers. To this end, he urged that every book of instruction for children be illustrated with woodcuts. Pictures of biblical scenes do not simply illustrate the text but are an integral part of the lesson, serving as the basis of discussion. And above all, the catechism must be a *narratio*, the telling of the story of creation, redemption and salvation. (While Fleury succeeded in explaining the Creed in the context of the history of salvation, his catechism was not greatly different from others of the time in its treatment of the Commandments and sacraments.)

2. Continuity and change in catechisms

Fleury cites Gregory of Nyssa's Great Catechism as a precedent for the longer catechisms (his own included) that were intended for the more educated. He does not, however, mention St Augustine's Enchiridion, *De Fide, Spe et Caritate*, which in fact established the basic structure for catechesis in the Middle Ages and which provided the outline for the later catechisms. The first and greatest part of the *Enchiridion* is an exposition of Christian faith based on the baptismal creed; the second part, develops the theme of hope based on the Lord's Prayer; and the third and briefest part (five short paragraphs) is a discourse on charity based on the twofold commandment of love—love of God and love of neighbour. (Augustine parallels the four stages of the Christian life—life according to the flesh, law, faith and the final resurrection—with four corresponding stages in salvation history—before the law, under the law, under grace and in full and perfect peace.) In the medieval period, the twofold commandment of love was explained in terms of the Decalogue. Catechisms, more intent on instruction than formation, lost sight of the virtues, putting the emphasis on the Creed, the Lord's Prayer and the Ten Commandments rather than faith, hope and charity as such.

Despite a certain formal (not to say, superficial) continuity that links modern texts with medieval catechesis and ancient works like Augustine's *Enchiridion*, the pattern of Catholic catechisms has changed greatly since the time of Fleury. Each period has shaped the catechism genre to its own needs and purposes. J. C. Dhôtel's study of the origins of the modern catechism describes how it assumed an apologetic role in combatting the teachings first of the Reformers and later of Jansenism and the Rationalists.[2] F. X. Arnold studied the influence of the Enlightenment on catechisms. Arnold found that in contrast to the catechisms of the sixteenth century which stressed the subjective appropriation of faith, post-Enlightenment catechisms emphasised the teaching of doctrinal formulas, determined more by philosophical considerations than by the economy of salvation. He cites the catechism of Giovanni Fabri (1558) which began by asking, 'Who is a Christian?' and contrasts it with eighteenth and nineteenth-century catechisms that began with questions like 'Who am I?' and 'Who made the world?' and 'Why was I created?'[3]

3. The push for uniformity

Pastoral needs encouraged a proliferation of catechisms, and pastoral concerns pushed for uniformity. The great Catholic reformers in France made the catechism a major concern. Vincent de Paul and Jean Eudes compiled catechisms for use in rural areas. Members of the Society of St Sulpice and the Community of Priests of St Nicholas-du-Chardonnet in Paris produced catechisms for use in catechetical institutes in urban settings. The desire to target catechisms to specific audiences and age groups, and (what is seldom mentioned) the interests and priorities of local bishops and religious communities like the Sulpicians and Ursulines, brought into existence a great number of catechetical works.

Bishops for their part tried to prevent the multiplication of catechisms. Dhôtel describes how Monsignor Hardoin de Péréfixe, Archbishop of Paris, promulgated the first diocesan catechism in France in 1659. He ordered that it be taught in all the churches, colleges, schools and catechetical centres of the archdiocese. Uniformity, however, proved elusive. In 1687, Péréfixe's successor was astonished at the variety of catechisms in use in Paris. To remedy the situation, he imposed a new one! (It was about this time that Fleury wrote his *Catéchisme historique*.) The problem endured and was compounded by the reorganisation of the dioceses under Napoleon. In 1806 Napoleon issued the infamous Imperial Catechism to be used in all the churches in the French empire, but with his fall, individual bishops began again to publish catechisms better adapted to the needs of their own dioceses.

The French influence in general and the Sulpician influence in particular, made itself felt in North America. In the vast territories that were to become part of the United States, bishops and missionaries produced catechisms in Indian dialects and for use on the American frontier. The English-speaking colonists had their Challoner ('The Penny Catechism'); the French, their Fleury; the Irish immigrants brought their Butler; the Germans, their Deharbe. The US bishops reacted against the proliferation of catechisms as early as 1829. The provincial Council of Baltimore condemned the 'promiscuous' use of unapproved catechisms and prayer books, and directed that a catechism adapted to the needs of American Catholics be prepared and issued with the approbation of the Holy See.[4]

In general the US bishops joined with those who gave enthusiastic support to the schema *De parvo catechismo* at the First Vatican Council. Their arguments for a universal catechism for children were based more on a desire for uniformity and central control, than on pedagogical and pastoral principles. In retrospect it is evident that if the decree *De parvo catechismo* had been implemented, the universal catechism of Vatican I would have been, like all catechisms before and since, a period-piece. It is likely that it would have looked very much like the Deharbe Catechism (1847) or Baltimore Catechism, commissioned by the US bishops a few years later (1884), both neo-scholastic works carrying the imprint of the Enlightenment.

Most of the bishops at Vatican I were disturbed by the great number of catechisms which they saw as a source of confusion. They overlooked the fact that the differences were more in the arrangement of material than in substance. In reality there were a few 'families' of catechisms whose origins could be traced to Canisius, Bellarmine, or one of the great post-Reformation authors. The catechisms that were products of the Enlightenment formed another family and were similar to one another in spirit and content.

4. National catechisms

The universal catechism envisaged by Vatican I never came into existence, but the twentieth century saw the spread of national catechisms: Pius X's *Compendio della dottrina cristiana* (1912) became the national catechism of Italy. The text published by Cardinal Amette for Paris (1914) became the national catechism of France in 1937. Belgium adopted a national catechism in 1945, Holland in 1948, Canada in 1951, Portugal in 1953, and Spain in 1960. They were intended primarily for use in schools. Although they differed in some minor ways, most followed the three-part outline popularised by Cardinal Pietro Gasparri's *Catechismus catholicus*—truths, duties, and means—published in 1930.

These catechisms met with criticisms almost as soon as they appeared. They did not take into consideration modern learning theory and the need to adapt textbooks to the age and background of the learner. Religious educators further criticised them for much the same reason that Fleury had faulted the catechisms of the seventeenth century: they did not clearly distinguish basic teachings from theological speculation. Their doctrine was safe, but they failed as catechetical texts for want of pastoral and pedagogical principles.

But it was not merely a question of method. The Catechetical Congress in Munich (1928) called for an improvement in the contents of the catechisms as well; more important than the 'how' of catechesis, was the 'what'. Although published after World War I, the national catechisms belonged more to the period of Vatican I. They largely ignored the new approaches to biblical studies and the spirit of the liturgical movement that had begun to transform Catholic life in the twentieth century. The first attempt to integrate kerygmatic theology, the Church's liturgical life, and modern pedagogy into a national catechism came with *Der katholische Katechismus*, published by the German hierarchy (1955) after almost twenty years of experimentation. Austria produced a national catechism along similar lines in 1960, and the *Catholic Catechism* issued by the Australian bishops in 1963–64 for use in the upper elementary grades was also modelled on the German work.

Despite the fact that it was translated into twenty-two languages within five years of its publication, the influence of *Der katholische Katechismus* outside Germany was short-lived. Its fate illustrates one of the limitations of all catechisms: they are time-bound. The German catechism was conceived and planned in 1938, and though modified and reworked in the years immediately following World War II, it is very much a product of the Church of Pius XII—systematic, complete and professional. On the other hand, it did not deal with social issues, which is a way of saying that it did not build on secular experience. By the time of John XXIII and the publication of *Mater et magister* and *Pacem in terris*, the German catechism was obsolete. The German catechism also illustrates another inherent limitation of the genre: Addressed to all believers *Der katholische Katechismus* was intended to be a family catechism, and when used (as catechisms often are) as a textbook in schools, it was found inadequate.

5. Vatican II and contemporary catechisms

The Second Vatican Council briefly considered commissioning a universal catechism, but instead mandated a 'directory' that would give general norms and principles for catechesis. In the spirit of Vatican II, the General Catechetical Directory, issued by the Congregation for the Clergy (1971) after consultation with national hierarchies throughout the Catholic world, accepted change and pluralism as positive values (nn. 2, 3), and recognises the legitimate desire of peoples to express the faith in their own idiom (n. 8). The GCD made 'catechesis for adults, since it deals with persons who are capable of an adherence that is fully responsible', normative for all forms of catechesis. Part III is an outline of 'The More Outstanding Elements of the Christian Message', but it says that 'in selecting a pedagogical method, one ought to take into account the circumstances in which the ecclesial community or the individuals among the faithful to whom the catechesis is directed live' (n. 46).

In the years immediately following Vatican II the spirit and principles of the General Directory encouraged new approaches to catechesis and gave rise to a new generation of catechisms. As the Council was drawing to a close, the Dutch bishops issued *De Nieuwe Katechismus*, intended primarily for adults (1965). It's phenomenal success in Holland and the English-speaking world, despite Rome's reservations, can only be explained by its timeliness. In one volume it presented Church teaching in the context of the much heralded 'new theology'. In 1970 the Italian bishops commissioned a *Catechismo per la vita cristiana*, that was to consist of a series of books addressed to different age groups from infancy to adulthood. The multi-volume work (1973–82) is the result of consultation with experts in scripture, liturgy, catechetics, psychology and theology, and feedback from catechists and parents. It has become the centrepiece in the work of renewing catechesis in Italy, providing direction for catechists and publishers of catechetical materials.

Two catechisms that have attempted to present the Christian message in a contemporary idiom have generated controversy. The one, a Latin American work, *Vamos Caminando*[5] ('Let Us Go Forward!'), was written by the pastoral team of Bombamarca, Peru. The methodology of liberation theology is evident in every unit: description and analysis of the local situation; reflection on that situation from a biblical or theological perspective; praxis—pastoral application and action. Although it was developed with the support of Peruvian bishops, the catechism has drawn criticism in some quarters, not because of doctrinal or moral teaching, but because of the prominent role it assigns to lay ministry in the local church.

In North America the most widely used adult catechism in the years after Vatican II was *Christ Among Us* by Anthony Wilhelm. It sold well over a million copies. Because of its popularity it attracted the notice of the Congregation for the Doctrine of the Faith, and the bishop of Newark, New Jersey who had given it the *imprimatur* was instructed to withdraw his approval. Several attempts were made to meet the objections of the Congregation, but in the end, Cardinal Ratzinger wrote that even with revisions Wilhelm's work would be unacceptable because of its 'methodology'. The SCDF, he said, 'does not agree that any work which cites individual theorists as though their views could supplant the teachings of the Church, can be described as a true catechetical text'.[6] (The 'theorists' in question were established theologians.)

About the same time that *Christ Among Us* was under scrutiny, the SCDF was also examining a text issued by the French bishops. In authorising the publication of *Pierres Vivantes* in 1981, the French bishops did not intend to issue a new catechism. None the less, because its purpose was to witness to the faith transmitted by the scriptures and the creeds, and because it was issued by the French episcopal conference, *Pierres Vivantes* was reviewed by the Congregation for the Doctrine of the Faith. A comparison of the original edition with the revised edition (1985) makes it clear that the Congregation's principle objection was again methodology. The 1981 version told the story of the People of God, beginning with

Exodus; the 1985 version begins with the story of creation and the fall. The 1981 version introduces the People of God in the New Testament with the Pentecost experience; the 1985 version introduces the New Testament with the infancy narratives.

Thus in tracing the evolution of catechisms from the sixteenth to the twentieth centuries, it is evident that the genre has taken on new significance. They have gradually become confessional documents in the tradition of Luther's Catechism, Heidelberg and Westminster. It has been clear since the seventeenth century that Catholic catechisms are expected to embody a corpus of doctrine that, however brief it is, presents an overview of what is considered at the time, complete and representative of the Catholic tradition. They have no set form or length and, until recently, they have not adhered to any one established way of presenting the Christian message. Canisius took one approach, Bellarmine another, Fleury suggested a third and the Enlightenment catechisms still another. All were acceptable and coexisted with the Tridentine Catechism which emphasised content more than method.

The Tridentine Catechism has been cited over and over again as the paradigm for the universal catechism commissioned by the Extraordinary Synod of Bishops in 1985. The new catechism will be to Vatican II what the *Catechismus ad parochus* was to Trent. One can only speculate what approach might have been taken had such a text been commissioned at Vatican II and the work given over to *periti* who had been participants in the Council. Most likely it would have been a very different document than the universal catechism now being compiled because the spirit of the sixties is different from the eighties, and the priorities of Pope Paul VI are different from those of Pope John Paul II.

Notes

1. *Catéchisme historique contenant en abrégé l'Historie Sainte et la Doctrine Chrétienne.*
2. J. C. Dhôtel, *Les origines du catéchisme moderne* (Paris 1967).
3. *Pastoraltheologische Durchblicke* (Freiburg im Briesgau 1965).
4. M. C. Bryce, *Pride of Place. The Role of the Bishops in the Development of Catechesis in the United States* (Washington 1984).
5. Pastoral Team of Bambamarca, *Vamos Caminando: A Peruvian Catechism* (Spanish 1977, ET London 1985).
6. *Origins: NC Documentary Service*, 14:28 (7 March 1985), p. 621.

Jürgen Werbick

Can the Universal Catechism Help Overcome the Crisis in Handing on the Faith?

IT WOULD certainly be unrealistic to hope that a universal catechism on its own would provide the turning-point in the crisis in the handing on of the faith that has occurred or become apparent throughout the world. But the catechism should be an aid (and for many theologians and church leaders the decisive aid) to remedy the uncertainty that is widely experienced by catechists and by all involved in handing on the faith and to give the transmission of the faith a reliable foundation once again. Indeed, a certain euphoria seems to be spreading that seriously endangers the whole project of a universal catechism by linking it to completely exaggerated expectations. What would thus seem to be indicated is an attempt on the basis of fundamental theology to clarify the function a catechism could have in the present crisis in handing on the faith and to indicate what should not be expected of it.

1. The crisis of tradition and the question of truth

For Archbishop J. J. Degenhardt of Paderborn a striking characteristic of the present crisis of tradition is that 'the question of the truth of the faith has in fact been quietly put into cold storage'. This neglect was expressed in a 'wide-spread ignorance of the faith among Christians themselves'. The 'fading knowledge of the content of the faith' must therefore be 'seriously considered'. If one started from the fact that the

idea of the faith as something definite and concrete was disappearing from
the consciousness of many people, that much that did not easily fit in with
modern ways of thought was left ill-defined and uncertain (Degenhardt
mentions the virgin birth, the resurrection, the ascension),[1] it seemed
reasonable to expect a catechism to give this definite and concrete quality a
sharper profile, to assert the truth of the faith that is determined by its
content. The question is only whether here one is not expecting to prove
the truth of the faith by merely establishing its identity—by authoritatively
establishing what can be called Christian. The tendency to equate
establishing the identity of the faith with proving its truth does not arise by
chance. 'Most theologians conduct their researches with the aim of securing
the identity of the Christian faith, not proving its truth', remarks G. Kegel,
perhaps not quite unjustly.[2]

Establishing the identity of the Christian faith could not be distinguished
from proving its truth as long as Christian faith was regarded as something
that could not be doubted because of its origins, with the result that what
demonstrably belonged to the faith seemed legitimated as true. Now
however the really decisive break in the history of Christianity that we at
present experience as the crisis of tradition is created by the fact that
Christian faith is no longer perceived as that which is automatically valid
on the basis of its origins but as an intellectual, philosophical and ethical
demand or imposition. The establishment of identity—the clarification of
the unabridged content of the faith, as can be expected from catechisms—
no longer provides anything directly for proving its truth. The question of
truth demands a process of proof which is to be provided not by showing
that it belongs to the authentic tradition of faith but by showing that it
belongs to the fundamental conditions of true humanity. What is 'tried and
tested' is no longer what already exists and is inherited from one's fathers
(and mothers) but that which survives the exchange of arguments in debate
by competent judges. And who does not feel himself or herself called to
join in debating and deciding questions of religion and philosophy!

Debate is meant to be a medium of emancipation: liberation from
unfounded claims to authority, liberation from what is apparently 'tried
and tested' (but only by tradition). Debate is meant to be the locus where
truth occurs because in it well-founded claims to truth can be proved to be
such. The hopeless utopianism of this model of proof has long since been
pointed out. Neither in scientific nor in everyday debate about the sense or
otherwise of traditions does one seem able really to do justice to what has
to be examined. Debate always seems to produce more arguments against
than for the validity of something that is possibly true or valid: criticism is
always stronger than confirmation because the criterion for criticism is

relatively easy to find and apply whereas on the other hand that for positive acceptance, especially in questions of religion and philosophy, is extraordinarily difficult. Arguments that establish the congruence of Christian faith and truly human life can only with difficulty be formulated convincingly because there is and indeed must be an endless dispute over what a truly human life should be. Thus the danger exists that debate, which has indeed established itself as virtually the reality of modern rationality in the consciousness of a 'critical' public, is continually critically eroding what Jürgen Habermas has called the 'resource of meaning', something that cannot be replenished at will, because it is hardly able to provide the legitimation or proof of proposed meanings or can only do so provisionally. The 'situation of a universal laboratory' of calling everything into question without reservation or exception seems to know only experiments aimed at falsifying ideas, so that the precarious possibility of an 'emancipation without meaning' emerges: 'Would it be possible one day for an emancipated human race to face itself in the enlarged arena of the formation of the will through discussion and debate and yet be deprived of the light in which it is capable of interpreting its life as something good?' That is Jürgen Habermas's question.[3] Does not the debate of those who are emancipating themselves from unproven claims to authority lead to more and more indifference, since it deprives of their unquestioned validity the hitherto valid criteria by which something had to demonstrate itself to be valid?

There was not long to wait for the reaction to the euphoria created by the idea of debate. A conservative attitude in the right sense, a protective attitude conserving of values (in E. Eppler's phrase) seemed called for not only with regard to natural resources but also with regard to resources of meaning: the slogan 'respect for what is there' made the rounds. But is not the heritage that is to be preserved in the religious field precisely that reserve of symbols of what C. G. Jung called the collective unconscious which makes the person growing up capable of a whole and 'holy' life if he or she is only sensitively opened up to it? The slogan 'respect for what is there', with which the Church's teaching authority, its pastors and catechists would be only too glad to agree, seems to overtake Christianity and leave it behind: Christianity appears as only one expression of what is eternally valid and laid down in the collective unconscious, not in any way as the only authoritative expression of this. Is Christian faith perhaps only true because and to the extent that the symbols of the collective unconscious can be re-discovered in it? It is clear that in this case Christianity would lose its identity. Hence the question: Can one prove the truth of the faith by establishing its identity?

The situation with regard to transmitting the faith has become complicated. As far at least as the churches of Western Europe and North America are concerned a very simplified version of things is as follows. Those handing on the faith can hardly hope that the contents of the faith can be clearly presented and accepted as rational without more ado in the critical debate of society; nor can they attach themselves unconditionally to the conservative reaction with its 'respect for what is there', because often enough this reaction leapfrogs over Christianity and seeks its salvation in the eternally valid truths of the collective unconscious. But in this case how can the proclamation of the faith and catechesis talk of the truth or truths of the faith in such a way that their reliability can emerge, that faith is capable of convincing and motivating people as the truth of salvation? Theology and the transmission of the faith should not begin by withdrawing from the modern situation of debate. But they can reflect and make it clear what kind of debate is suitable for the faith's claim to truth; and they will go on trying to show how superficially falsifying arguments criticising Christianity involve a short-circuit and to do the same for failed attempts to refute the truth of the faith.

2. Bearing convincing witness to the truth of the faith in a way that will also motivate people

Simply repeating and expounding what belongs to the Christian faith, what indissolubly characterises it, is certainly not enough. Handing on the faith must convince; and it will only convince if it clearly and at least provisionally makes it possible to experience how faith calls into question at the deepest level those investigating it, how, for their salvation, it enables them to think, to live and to act, and how it inspires them to an intense hope that is at the same time well-founded.

A catechism that is meant to serve this kind of handing on of the faith would need to contribute to making convincing witness possible and would therefore need to be conceived of as a way of introducing people to the experience of those who believe, in other words to be mystagogic, since it is only from the living experience of faith that convincing witness can emerge. For this reason Herbert Vorgrimler has proposed that the universal catechism should 'bundle together particular testimonies of faith from every possible situation in which believers find themselves'.[4] This idea remains justified even if it is not easy to imagine how it can be reconciled with the literary form of a catechism. Traditionally the catechism is rather a compendium of doctrine for the 'simple faithful'. One ought to be able to expect of such a doctrinal compendium that aims at mystagogy that it elucidates the doctrine of the faith as a pointer towards and an exposition of the specifically Christian experience of the faith. The minimum condition for this would probably be that the readers actually understand the doctrine of the faith that is offered, that they find it a valid exposition of their experience of life, their conflicts and dilemmas, their failures and their longings. It is as a valid exposition of human life in all its dimensions and with regard to all its decisive alternatives that the doctrine of the faith can prove itself, can convince them and be handed on in witness that carries conviction.

The locus for conviction in faith and conviction directed towards faith is that everyday discussion and debate, only exceptionally conducted on methodical and scientific principles, about the all-determining orientation of life and about that which ultimately determines its reality. In this, alongside the relevance of faith for the interpretation of human life, its inner consistency—the *nexus mysteriorum* that enables each mystery of the faith to develop and disclose the authentically Christian experience of God—is of course examined, as well as the extent to which it is rooted in the original Christian testimonies and authoritative traditions. To this extent, then, establishing the identity of the faith is a factor in the demonstration of its validity. This debate is conducted first of all by those who find themselves in the Christian tradition and wish to give a responsible account of what has been handed on to them. To this extent it is not without prior conditions and presuppositions, but in principle it is open to all the questions and questionings of what is Christian in the religious and philosophical debate of the contemporary world. Precisely in its openness it presupposes the testimony of those who experience Christian faith as viable and accountable, and it is itself the precondition for free assent to the faith and freely given witness.

Testimony will only be convincing if it makes visible the free conviction of the witness: if it makes visible that the witness vouches for what he or she believes not through pressure, whether internal or external, not because of convention or the sheep-like acceptance of what has been handed on, but simply because he or she has tested it and found it to carry conviction. When in testimony a process of conviction becomes visible it can encourage testing the ability to convince of what is being testified to. But is it not here that the actual dilemma of the contemporary crisis of tradition is to be found: in the fact that the witness borne by believers often betrays a bad intellectual conscience; in the fact that many believers shy away from the all-too-bright light of critical publicity with a sacrifice of the intellect which they think they have to make for the sake of their faith? Anyone active in adult education can confirm this anew in any establishment. The central truths of the faith are perceived as things that have to be believed only with very mixed feelings precisely by members of congregations who are actually interested in their church membership; one would sooner not be seen as someone who still believes all that. And is it not a colossal intellectual cheek to hold to be true the teachings of the catechism that are simply repeating traditional formulae and patterns of thought—as for example in the much praised catechism of the German dioceses published in the 1950s—on salvation and original sin, on the trinity, on the two natures of Jesus Christ, on the last judgment and the everlasting life of the redeemed? Is this always simply the stumbling-block and folly of the cross which those who believe have to confess and maintain against the wisdom of this world?

Certainly it cannot be a question of reducing the demands of the faith to what is currently plausible, to let the question of a new and fulfilled life beyond individual death rest with the cheap 'argument' that nobody can believe that any more. But it must therefore be a question of refusing to allow unnecessary intellectual claims to smother the true challenge of the faith, the demand to trust more in the God of love and in love for his sake than in any other power and to entrust him with the completion of our damaged life that is doomed to failure. These intellectual claims that profoundly unsettle many of the faithful are frequently due to a form of the doctrine of the faith whereby a particular doctrine could to some extent be made comprehensible in terms of a particular culture and within the assumptions generally shared at that time and place (compare, for example, the idea of satisfaction, the psychological doctrine of the trinity, the doctrine of transubstantiation). Attempts of this kind to lead people to understand what they believe become serious obstacles to understanding once the assumptions that used to be taken for granted have collapsed. Certainly theologians have the task of working out what was 'really meant' in these original formulations and to express it afresh. But they can only do this within a new paradigm, a new and risky attempt that will certainly also be one-sided and may well possibly fail to grasp and understand the *nexus mysteriorum* anew.

The proposed universal catechism, however, is not intended to be a fallible theological exercise of this kind. Its aim is merely to present 'sound' church Doctrine, while admittedly being 'adapted to the modern outlook of believers'.[5] But there can be no question of adapting or adjusting the doctrine to the modern outlook. Rather it is the modern world that has to be adapted to the gospel: as H. Vorgrimler has said, it needs at least to be called into question on the basis of the gospel and reminded of its purpose.[6] But this calling into question and challenge must be capable of being understood by it; and that is precisely what is lacking. Doctrine does not become a challenge if, because of all the possible avoidable obstacles to understanding, it merely causes confused irritation and hence is met with indifference and apathy. It only becomes a challenge if it convincingly lays bare fundamental alternatives in view of which one can reach a conscious and free decision. And it makes possible a testimony that motivates, that is contagious, if the doctrines of the faith are developed 'as formulas of a dangerous and liberating memory, as histories abbreviated to formulas and to a certain extent expressed in shorthand', histories 'of departure and conversion, of resistance and suffering', of discovery and discipleship.[7] Debate about the extent to which Christianity is proven and reliable will continually be transformed into the narrative making present of these histories. It is only in this way, and not through the mere repetition of traditional 'sound' doctrine, that the dangerous memory of suffering and salvation, the commemoration of God as the one who can be called on in suffering and jointly with the sufferer, becomes alive in the present.

Using the term 'adaptation' promises too much and will retain too little: it feeds the illusion that the faith, as it is to be presented in the catechism, could perhaps be understood by itself in the future; and, I am afraid, it will achieve only halfheartedly what makes those who believe capable of giving convincing and motivating witness, that is expressing the truth of the faith from its core as a challenge to modern man and as a 'dangerous memory', in J. B. Metz's phrase. That demands a bold and risky theological and kerygmatic enterprise that is threatened with failure. But the person who withdraws into the calm zone of sound doctrine that is free not only of storms but also of discussion and tension, the zone of what W. Kasper has described as 'Mother Church's original key', decidedly risks too little and is in danger of wanting to make it possible to demonstrate, merely by safeguarding its identity, the truth of the faith and its being borne witness to in convincing testimony.

3. Bearing credible witness to the faith

A further reason for the obvious problems with handing on the faith seems to be the profound crisis of credibility which is currently affecting the Church, along with all other traditional institutions, but which displays quite specific characteristics in its case. The Church deprives itself of credibility whenever its interest in asserting itself forces into the background the witness that provides the meaning of its existence, whenever the calculus of power leads it away from the side of those whom Jesus had in mind in the beatitudes. The dominance of thinking in terms of power and self-assertion naturally has a theological and kerygmatic dimension too; and it is displayed here as a refusal in practice to enter into argument on important questions of the life of the Church and of faith. To take three examples at random: first, the ordination of women and allowing lay people to give the homily at the eucharist are rejected with arguments which because of their obvious inadequacy are for the most part perceived as a cover-up for refusal to enter into discussion. The papal decision on birth control in the encyclical *Humanae vitae* did not take the trouble seriously to examine and to refute the arguments of the majority of the commission of experts that had previously been set up. Thus there arose the extremely damaging impression for the credibility of the Church as an institution that there was only one serious reason for these decisions: the need to protect at any price the continuity of doctrinal tradition—the preservation of identity whatever the situation with regard to the actual arguments. The minority on the commission of experts said this quite explicitly and openly.[8]

The history of the reception of the encyclical *Humanae vitae* shows clearly enough how the credibility of the Church's teaching authority is damaged when in this way the preservation of identity is placed above care and respect for the actual arguments. Anyone who refuses to become involved in debate and in the work of conviction with arguments that clarify and develop the case is only able to appeal to obedience. Obedience attained in this way depends on bad intellectual consciences that have been more or less successfully suppressed; but the climate of suppression is the worst conceivable pre-condition for a witness based on conscientious conviction, for the handing on of the faith in a way that motivates people and aims at free identification with it.

Anyone who becomes involved in debate—and in the long term no other choice is open to the Church's teaching authority—must take his or her partner in dialogue seriously as a partner competent to join in the discourse in the business of discovering and establishing the truth. Can the Church become involved in this way when it is itself entrusted with administering the *depositum fidei*? The answer is that it has to, since the truth of the faith is shown in its significance, viability and dependability only in the way of life, in the experience of the faith, and in the reflection and thought of the many who believe; and this truth is expressed instructively in witness, whereby individual believers tell each other how faith becomes fruitful and meaningful in their lives, what it means for them, what it gives them to think, to hope and to do. Handing on the faith will probably only still take place successfully if teenagers enter into this debate and are able to have a voice in it and if believers are 'addressed not primarily as objects but as subjects or agents, not as an audience but above all as bearers of the faith

and of the remembrance of God'.[9] Catechisms will promote the handing
on of the faith when they also encourage this business of becoming subjects
and agents in the faith, if they deal with the debate in which believers bear
witness and in this articulate the doctrine of the Church as a helpful request
to enter the debate while also marking out the basic points of orientation
without which this debate must lack any sense of direction. The fact that
this is not a utopian demand is shown by the adult catechism of the United
Evangelical-Lutheran Church of Germany, a catechism dedicated to
achieving this end.

4. Proclamation and witness

But does not Catholic ecclesiology demand that official proclamation
should be ranked above the 'witness-debate' of those who believe and those
who are seeking the truth of the faith? Documents of the Church's teaching
authority, such as the *Instrumentum laboris* (§ 18) for the 1987 Synod of
Bishops, contrast the preaching carried out with doctrinal authority by the
Church's office-holders with the unofficial witness to the faith of the laity;
and this contrast is used among other things to justify the ban on lay
preaching. Now there is certainly no doubt that proclamation too must be
witness if it is to convince and that therefore it cannot position itself outside
the 'witness-debate' of the faithful. But if nevertheless it tried to do that
and wanted to confine itself to making known what is meant to be pure
and 'sound' doctrine it would become increasingly meaningless for the lived
faith of members of the community because it would have lost its
relationship to this. An effort to adapt to modern ways of thinking would
then come too late and would be hardly more than a clumsy attempt to
curry favour.

It should also of course be undisputed that within the 'witness-debate'
there should and must be a variety of different roles in the dialogue,
including the role of those whose aim is to examine from the point of view
of how Christian it is the witness of believers in deed and word and the
theological framework that this witness intends to make possible: the role
in fact of those whose vocation and mission it is to establish the identity of
the faith, those entrusted with the Church's teaching authority. The
establishment of identity is only one task, even if also a central one, in the
'witness-debate' of the community of those who believe. It is indispensable.
It is indispensable because there must be an authority which decides if a
proposed theological or kerygmatic framework or a form of witness no
longer deserves the name of Christian—in which case the burden of proof
would in every single case fall on those who deliver this verdict. Official

Church doctrine, as for example it is more or less comprehensively collected in Denzinger, is the crystallised deposit of past instances of this kind of establishment of identity or the reverse in critical situations in the history of the Church and of dogma, as well as of the not always successful attempts to provide a positive justification of these decisions. A catechism ought not to confine itself to recapitulating and defending this doctrine. It can and should certainly have the function of introducing in an understandable form into the 'witness-debate' the criteria for establishing identity. But if it confined itself to this it would be primarily an instrument for delimiting boundaries. But proclaiming and handing on the faith is not primarily a business of safeguarding the faithful from dubious and ambiguous doctrines, even if for many theologians and church leaders it seems above all to be a question of drawing boundaries to shut out dangerous rivals[10] and 'syncretistic aberrations'. In view of the number of different philosophies on offer today it may well be an urgent necessity to give what is specifically Christian a higher profile; but here the fixing of boundaries and fencing things off is only superficially helpful. What is specifically Christian will emerge when the core of the Christian faith can be articulated in such a way that people see themselves brought face to face with the fundamental alternatives of their lives and inserted within the liberating remembrance of God in the history of God's dealings with mankind. This, however, can only take place within the context of a living, challenging 'witness-debate' in which those taking part tell each other how their faith challenges them and what decisions it demands of them, as well as the hope with which they put themselves on the road of discipleship. It is this debate and not just fencing things off that a universal catechism must serve if it is to help overcome the crisis of handing on the faith.

Translated by Robert Nowell

Notes

1. *Cf.*, J. J. Degenhardt, 'Tradierungskrise des Glaubens', in E. Feifel and W. Kasper (ed.), *Tradierungskrise des Glaubens*, (Munich 1987), pp. 11–29: p. 20.
2. At the start of his *Und ich sah einen neuen Himmel und eine neue Erde. Das Neue Testament und die Heilung der Welt* (Gütersloh 1988, p. 11), a work weak in argument and extravagant in the theses it puts forward.
3. J. Habermas, *Bewußtmachende oder rettende Kritik—die Aktualität Walter Benjamins: Zur Aktualität Walter Benjamins* (Frankfurt am Main 1972), pp. 173–223: pp. 219–220.
4. H. Vorgrimler, 'The Adventure of a New "World Catechism" ', *Concilium* 192 (Edinburgh 1987), 103–109, 105.

5. *Zukunft aus der Kraft des Konzils. Die außerordentliche Bischofssynode '85. Die Dokumente mit einem Kommentar von W. Kasper* (Freiburg im Breisgau), p. 31.

6. *Cf.*, note 5 above.

7. *Cf.*, J. B. Metz, 'Wohin ist Gott, wohin denn der Mensch?', in F. X. Kaufmann and J. B. Metz, *Zukunftsfähigkeit. Suchbewegungen im Christentum* (Freiburg im Breisgau 1987), pp. 124–147: p. 145.

8. 'The Birth Control Report: II: The Conservative Case', *The Tablet*, 29 April 1967, pp. 478–485: p. 480. The document—first published with the other texts of the papal commission on birth control by the *National Catholic Reporter* in April 1967—is also to be found in Peter Harris *et al.*, *On Human Life: An Examination of 'Humanae Vitae'* (London 1968), pp. 170–202, with the passage referred to on pp. 181–182.

9. For more detailed treatment see my article 'Religionsdidaktik als "theologische Konkretionswissenschaft"' in *Katechetische Blätter* 113 (1988), 82–99. The quotation is taken from J. B. Metz, 'Suchbewegungen nach einem neuen Gemeindebild', in F. X. Kaufmann and J. B. Metz, *Zukunftsfähigkeit* (cited in note 7 above), pp. 148–165: p. 150.

10. *Cf.*, for example, W. Kasper, 'Tradierung und Vermittlung als systematisch-theologisches Problem', in E. Feifel and W. Kasper, *Tradierungskrise des Glaubens* (cited in note 1 above), pp. 30–52: p. 34.

Hermann Häring

Experiences with the 'Short-Formula' of the Faith

NEW ERAS, even short-lived ones, try to find their own forms of speech and their own formulas. Their meaning and their function often only become clear in retrospect. In 1965 Karl Rahner made the attempt to express the Christian faith in a short summary which could be generally understood: in an age of growing secularization it was of vital importance 'to present the essence of the Christian faith in language which could be understood by non-believers'.[1] In 1967 Rahner published a revised form of his draft statement in *Concilium*. Finally in 1970 he returned to the subject in the light of the lively discussion which had arisen in the meantime. This time he produced three formulas—described as 'theological', 'sociological' (later 'anthropological') and 'futurological'—which, according to his own interpretation, have a trinitarian structure. Rahner incorporated this article almost unchanged, as a 'little epilogue', into his later work *Grundkurs des Glaubens*.[2] It is clear that the project was of great importance to Rahner himself. Has it awakened an echo elsewhere?

At first it seemed as though there would be a great future for the undertaking, since the original article did in fact provoke a lively response, especially in German-speaking countries. Systematic theologians like H. Küng[3] and Th. Schneider,[4] pastoral theologians and teachers of religion like H. Schuster,[5] A Stock[6] and R. Bleistein,[7] and exegetes like F. Mussner,[8] among others, all took up the discussion. As early as 1967 F. Varillon produced an Outline of the Catholic faith.[9] J. Ratzinger[10] reacted with caution, in view of the generally binding nature of the creeds. K. Lehmann, approaching the question from the angle of his New Testament

61

studies, was able to strike a balance between different points of view,[11] but produced no formula of his own. At the same time the question of short-formulas became part of a wider framework—that of the renewal and reformulation of creeds in general. In this connection we should think not only of the 'Credo of the People of God', issued by Paul VI in June 1968,[12] but of all the efforts produced both in Evangelical churches and in the Catholic Church in many countries, by church groups, and even at the level of the World Council of Churches.[13] L. Karrer gathers together all the intensive discussion in a comprehensive monograph.[14] It is not by chance that this arises from catechetical and religious educational concerns.

Meanwhile the formal interest in short-formulas has receded considerably. But this does not mean that the matter has been disposed of. In the first part of this study, therefore, we shall address ourselves to the discussion initiated by Rahner. The second part takes up the particular interest and problem of short-formulas. In the third part we suggest some conclusions which arise from the 'short-formula' project in comparison with new credal formulas. It may be stated at this point that these investigations do not lend support to the idea of a 'world catechism'.

1. The development of the discussion: is the project clear?

(a) Communication with those outside: the 'unbelievers'

K. Rahner's personal starting-point is clear. At a time when the Catholic Church is beginning to think about its relationship with the 'world of today' (cf. the Pastoral Constitution *Gaudium et spes*), some guidance should be offered to those without any prior knowledge or any Christian background who ask for some basic statement of the essential content of the Christian faith. Rahner speaks of unbelievers. The word 'unbelieving' is for him in the first place a cultural-social expression, and is applied to those who, under present-day conditions, are strangers to the (Christian) faith. Therefore Rahner is looking for formulations which (a) dispense with the current vocabularly of Christian creeds, without thereby losing the content; which (b) therefore are immediately intelligible to non-Christians; and which especially (c) take account of the particular situation of a secularized society. A short-formula of the faith can no longer take the word 'God' for granted, but must first explain what is meant by 'God'. In addition, in view of the critical-historical consciousness, talk of Jesus Christ must be safeguarded against possible mythical misunderstandings. In this way

Rahner aims at a restrained introduction which will open the way to understanding for those who are far off. We cannot therefore speak of an objectivising treatment, using advertising techniques (Ratzinger[15]). But that means that with his short-formula Rahner is practising apologetics and communication in the best sense of those words.

(b) Understanding for those inside: catechesis

It is obvious that the first reactions very quickly revealed that it was not only the 'unbelievers' who needed fresh guidance and a clarification of Christian belief. In a secular society, unbelief has become a structural phenomenon whose presuppositions and vocabulary are common to Christians and atheists alike. The new attempt to communicate with those outside therefore requires a fundamental new orientation for those inside. That explains why Rahner, in a work which appeared in 1970, reflects on the general cultural conditioning of the West, and on the situation of the Church in Western society. Constant exposure to stimuli, the rapid pace of life, pluralism, alienation from God, existential questionings, criticisms of an objectivistic and monolithic theology—all these come into one's sights, as does the general experience that current confessions of faith require so much interpretation that they have lost their immediacy, and no longer have any power to convince.[16]

Therefore such a formula must not only take account, in a productive way, of present-day conditions, but must also be suitable for catechetical use within the Church (Rahner: it must be capable of assimilation by spirit, heart and memory), must take into consideration the cultural variety of the world Church, and must display a critical capacity for concentrating on what is important for concrete Christianity.[17] We are now concerned with much more than a question of good translation. It is a fundamental matter of hermeneutics in present-day language for the Christian faith, and of a fresh formulation of its central content. When it is seen in this way, Rahner's call is evidence of a newly-awakened self-confidence in critical theology.

(c) Differentiation and confession

This theologically differentiating element then determines the course of the wider discussion. Short-formulas must, in the end, give expression to the heart of the Christian gospel itself, and must distinguish critically between what is important and what is unimportant, between statements of general significance and theological niceties. The person who believes must not only plainly confess, but also know what and in whom he believes. Credal formulations must therefore be clearly different from other ideological conceptions. Thus Rahner ends by placing this undertaking firmly in the centre of contemporary theological questions, and observes 'that the apostolic confession of faith, especially the baptismal confession of those baptised as adults, had such a function, and that indeed such short credal formulations are to be found in the New Testament'. With reference to the 'hierarchy of truths' (*Unitatis redintegratio* 11), he asks for a clear structuring of statements of faith, as protection against an amorphous mass of individual statements, and against a religious praxis which dissipates its energies in secondary concerns. He asks also that the Christian lay person, who, though he is not an academic theologian, must nevertheless be able to answer for his faith in his non-Christian environment, should have at his disposal such a short formulation of his faith and his belief—a formulation centred on what is really important.[18] The decisive elements of post-conciliar theology are brought together here: inspiration from the New Testament, a new discovery of elementary expressions of faith, a structuring of the sum total of 'truths' handed down,[19] the maturity of the laity, pastoral intentions and self-restraint on the part of professional theology. The question which had seemed to be about non-believers had turned into a question about what was distinctively Christian.

(d) Reference to Jesus Christ

Alongside the question as to what was really important, there arose a concern for brevity and precision. Rahner, who at first regards the length of a full confession of faith as acceptable, ends by restricting himself to three pregnant formulas which are further abbreviated in the course of pedagogical discussion.[20] Determinative for this development is, of course, the positive recognition of the abundance in the New Testament of short confessional formulas, any of which may be regarded as a summary of the whole Christian faith. There is therefore no lack of proposals that such New Testament formulas should be directly brought back into use as short statements of contemporary faith. Lehmann reminds us of Exodus formulas from the Old Testament,[21] and of the expression 'I your God—you my people' (Deut. 16:17); Mussner of 1 John 3:23: 'And this is his commandment, that we should believe in the name of his Son Jesus Christ, and love one another, just as he has commanded us'.[22] These (counter-) proposals not only have this biblical immediacy, but they represent an attempt to relate particular systematic theological presuppositions to their biblical origins.[23] For this reason, and because of the pressing question as to what is distinctively Christian, other attempts are centred on discipleship of Jesus Christ, with the closest possible direct reference to him. According to H. Küng, the Christian gospel is perhaps expressed 'in one word, Jesus as the Christ . . . Only that person, or activity, or church is Christian which is related to Christ, or, better, which follows Jesus Christ.' It is on this basis that Küng produces three formulas of his own, the first of which is used later as the conclusion of his book *Christ sein* (ET *On Being A Christian*).[24] This development represents a carrying out of Rahner's original intention—but only in part, since the 'content' of the Christian message, what the Christian message is about, is again replaced either by biblical formulas or through a 'confessing' reference to Jesus Christ. Thus there has been a shift not only in the starting-point, but also in the inner dimension of the short-formula. We cannot speak of a clearly-defined project: 'Short-formulas of the faith'.

2. The question at issue: the logic of Christianity

(a) A subject for theologians

The quest for short-formulas of the faith is to be understood in the light of the post-conciliar situation in progressive theology. This theology had achieved only partial success in its attempt to create conditions throughout the whole Church under which the reform of the Church might be begun, Scripture might be recognised as the 'soul of theology', relations with non-Catholic churches might be regulated on a basis of partnership, and the modern world might be taken seriously for what it really is. This basic work was not completed by the Council, and it was increasingly impeded by conservative forces. It was vitally necessary, therefore, for theology to come to an understanding of its own responsibility for its terms of reference, and therefore for the inner structure and rationality of the Christian faith, and to articulate the faith as appropriately as possible in terms of present-day thinking. Only in that way could it justify and authenticate itself.

Therefore, from the beginning, central investigations into God, Christ and Church, and into the basic anthropological and political dimensions of the faith, have been working in opposition to the explosive multiplicity of post-conciliar themes.[25] Theologically speaking, the *aggiornamento* does not lead to fashionable novelties, but to the renewing of the formulations. It is important, as ecclesiastical opposition develops, to discover afresh, in the light of discussions going on at that moment in the whole Church, precisely what—at the heart of things—it is all about. Against this background, the specifically theological concern of the basic formulas is understandable: to discover, and in the light of present conditions to formulate afresh, is not just a matter of a new, or revised, symbol of the faith, but of the inner logic and structure of the Christian gospel itself. This reveals not only, as indicated above, a coincidence of internal church interests and apologetic ones, but also the main purpose of theology, which is to be the spokesperson for internal reform in the Church.

That means, however, that reflection on the inner logic and structure of the faith can only be begun within the framework of a scientifically orientated dialogue. If we wish to further the process of *aggiornamento*, we must argue competently, teach effectively, and put forward cogent arguments for discussion. It is precisely for this reason that it can never be the immediate aim of theology to create a new binding consensus. Short-formulas were not and are not ecclesiastical confessions. No; they must begin as particular propositions of individual theologians, and be argued about, criticised and corrected.

(b) Three different starting-points

At the same time the question naturally arises as to how reconcilable may be the theological concepts lying behind formulas which may be proposed. Superficially the formulas appear very similar. God is presented always as the ground and goal of human existence, Christ as the measure and distinctive content of the Christian faith, trust and love in the community of the decisive expressions of Christian praxis. But the inner life of the formulas, their inner structure and argumentation, are very different. Alongside simple re-presentations of traditional confessions of faith, we can mention three such concepts, dating from before 1970, which cannot be reconciled:

(a) The exegete goes back directly to the short-formulas in the New Testament, and chooses one which seems to him particularly suited to the present time. In doing this he aligns himself with the uncontested stream of the tradition of the whole Church, and so is convinced that he is steering clear of modern theological deviations.[26] Of course he has great difficulty in justifying his choice. Strictly speaking he remains within an area of discussion which may be Christian but is pre-scientific, and is, in principle, no different from a biblicist approach.

(b) The 'fundamental theologian' (if I may be permitted to describe Rahner in this way) makes his own basic theological theory in the heart of the Christian gospel: God appears as the enabler and the goal of human transcendence. In Jesus Christ, says the further explanation, this goal is positively attained. Christianity keeps the question of the absolute future in Christ open, but realises it here and now in Church and sacrament.[27] Thus the basic affirmation of the Christian understanding of God is ontologically established but conveyed in a defining (no longer historical) way. Moreover, this formula, which is radically open to the universality of salvation, depends for its formulation and exposition directly on Rahner's transcendental-theological presuppositions, which as such cannot be regarded as part of the common Christian tradition. In outward appearance, Rahner is therefore no different in principle from other speculative approaches linked with particular philosophical presuppositions.

(c) The biblically and historically orientated systematic theologian (if we may classify H. Küng in this way) reconstructs the person, message and life-story of Jesus of Nazareth, and makes it the basis for all wider theological thinking, so as to relate it (bringing historical recollection and present Easter faith together) to the discipleship of present-day Christians. In such discipleship (runs the central thesis), we can have a genuinely human life and death in freedom from hostile powers, idols and false gods, and we can call on God as our Father.[28] In this formula, which most clearly distinguishes what is Christian, the element of remembrance in the Christian faith comes directly into play. Of course, in discussion of its hermeneutical and topical presuppositions, questions are asked precisely at the point which it regards as crucial: the correlation between praxis and theory. Does Küng's formula offer a fundamental counterbalance to the ideological distortions of modern preaching and morality?

Thus each of the three approaches is most vulnerable precisely at the point which it is trying to defend. Taken together they show that there is scarcely any active consensus in the area of scientific communication. Therefore they not only need to be mutually complemented and corrected: they also need an agreed common basis of understanding. What sort of common basis could that be? An unexpected answer was provided by the *Concilium* World Congress in Brussels in 1970.[29]

(c) Concilium 1970

In this Congress Catholic theology revealed a self-confidence rarely seen in modern times. Theology must, said W. Kasper on the first day, constantly translate the gospel afresh for the present day. Theology is concerned with the discerning of spirits, with the 'humanising of the application of the faith and of the life of the Church', and thus with the 'present-day relevance of Christianity'. The speaker therefore called for a 'dynamic and dialogic understanding of orthodoxy', and an 'open and public dialogue with all charisms, offices and trends in the Church.' In all this, theology must constantly run the risk of error, and work through all conceivable possibilities, in order to seek out future directions for the Church. So theology can 'sabotage the attitude of resignation which is creeping into the Church at the present time, and the resultant closed mentality, not open to renewal, by which the Church's mission—to be a sign of hope for mankind—is betrayed'.[30]

After the question of the basic formula had been raised on the second day, and answered by three speakers with astonishing unanimity,[31] on the third day the subject for discussion was: 'The Church's "present" in society's "tomorrow"', for which theologians too have a responsibility.[32] Only in retrospect can it be seen how explosive this subject could be. Is it, then, pastorally engaged theologians who, as the qualified theoreticians of Christianity, direct and guarantee the future of the Church in the world of tomorrow? Let us stay with the Congress. This idea was challenged dialectically at three points:

First with the assertion that, strictly speaking, the notion of a professional theologian is a blasphemy, and that all Christians are therefore theologians.[33] The dominance of (fundamental) theological theorising (Rahner's formula) is thereby challenged. New basic theories of the faith must be supported by the whole Church, that is by all Church members.

Secondly with the assertion that only a Church and theology in solidarity with the world can carry out their task correctly.[34] The danger of biblicism (Mussner's formula) is thereby checked. The translating of Scripture has to be done within the framework of the contemporary world and contemporary cultures.

Thirdly with the political-theological thesis that the Christian gospel and the church need to break away from their privatised and ideologically suspect understanding, and to interpret God's new thing as a story of liberation.[35] The open-ended thought of discipleship (Küng's formula) is thereby given an eschatological interpretation. The remembrance of Jesus Christ leads to the Kingdom of freedom.

(d) Towards theological solidarity

Of course all these statements remain theoretical, and have therefore developed one-sidedly, starting from theory and moving towards practical application. This is evident from the complaint of many who were present that—in spite of its attempts to be socially engaged—the Congress had remained in the ivory tower of Western academic thinking. It is true that there was theoretical reflection on the presence of the Church in present and future society; it is true that the need for enlightenment within the Church, and enlightened self-criticism, was called for. But a large number of participants were not satisfied with this modern Western thought-strategy. They were convinced that theology and its central affirmations could only achieve the humanising power demanded by W. Kasper when the thought-process was reversed, so that it proceeded from praxis to theory—when, that is to say (and always within the concept of liberating discipleship), its answers were derived fresh from concrete situations in the Church and in society, and were unmistakably related to them. Thus a concrete analysis of the economic and political structures of society and Church is called for, with a view to man's radical liberation. Solidarity is urged with all those who, in the struggle for human liberation, have found themselves threatened, imprisoned, tortured or exiled.[36] Through their testimony alone could the liberating power become reality. Liberation theology has been the first of the emancipatory theologies which have arisen to claim its right to speak among Catholic theologians.

Thus, unexpectedly, and unnoticed by many, the Congress was a signal of the new orientation. It was possible to see in it where a theology leads when it does its reflection, under the conditions of present-day reality, on the inner logic and structure of the Christian message. A theology rising from such a foundation could no longer be confined to questions of the inner life of the Church, because it discovers the challenge of a torn humanity, and a complex world controlled by deadly powers. It must now stop being the one and only, Western dominated (and male dominated) theology.[37] The decisive experience of this Congress was that short-formulas of the faith do not become effective by their own strength, that they cannot of themselves create consensus, and that they cannot by virtue of their own authority develop a consensus binding on the Church. They only become effective when—in their confession of God, of Jesus Christ and of the Spirit of fellowship, whoever might contest it—they take account of present-day reality, interpret it by the standard of the Kingdom of God, and live by their solidarity with those who fight and suffer for human liberation. It goes without saying that criticism of the defects of the Church as it actually exists is not by-passed, but included.

3. Short-formula and creed

(a) Who formulates Christian truth?

The discussion about short-formulas of the faith, carried on in those days by a progressive wing of Catholic theology, naturally led to argument between those holding different theological and ecclesiastical views. From this some further clarifications have resulted, important among which are the articles of J. Ratzinger. In the light of different kinds of symbols,[38] he assigns to short-formulas, as to baptismal symbols, a (pre-)catechetical function. At the same time they can, like ordination symbols (such as the Athanasian), 'compress' together theological statements at the level of theological reflection. A theologically and culturally conditioned plurality is therefore legitimate. In each case these short-formulas are formulas of reflection on the faith, and therefore 'exegesis of statements'. It is noteworthy that Ratzinger removes short-formulas from the category of catechesis to that of 'pre-catechesis'. But we would have no complaint against Ratzinger's analysis if he had not abruptly added the comment that symbols are not exegesis, but 'the thing itself'. 'While the baptismal symbol sets out, without any commentary, the important facts of the faith as such, these texts offer not the facts of the faith, but reflection (!) on those facts.'[39]

This distinction is too simple. Of course short-formulas cannot in the strict sense replace the creeds (which is what Ratzinger seems to fear). They are rather, from a catechetical point of view, outposts of the creeds in a non-Christian world, and, from a fundamental theological point of view, a way in to criticism within theology, and to Christian decision making. That does not mean, however, that symbols themselves are reflection-free, and, as it were, pre-theological, and so are to be carefully separated from short-formulas.[40] But in his discussion of the conciliar symbols Ratzinger makes one point very clearly. As a point of reference for preaching and episcopal oversight, they are an essential 'instrument for the unity of the whole Church'. A creed is 'what the Church, above and beyond all changes in theological interpretation, has identified as the authentic word of faith ("Dogma")'.[41] At points of disagreement, therefore, he sets dogma over against theological statements. It is thus a question of the tension between the claims of theology and church leadership respectively to formulate Christian truth. It is a question of the difference between rational and traditional methods of argument. In all this Ratzinger overlooks the third component, which should take precedence over both theological reflection and episcopal oversight: the praxis of the Christian life, hoping for liberation in many different forms. It is only out of this Christian life that Christian confession and ecclesiastical consensus can develop.

(b) Creeds as an example

Short-formulas of the faith have over and over again resulted from the inadequacy of traditional creeds and the incomprehensibility of many articles of faith. They have therefore, like theology as a whole, a subsidiary yet indispensable function. That is why no theologian has made the claim that he can replace a creed with a theological formula, though the boundaries are fluid. But it would also be presumptuous to expect renewal simply from reflection and criticism. Now it has happened that in recent decades not only short-formulas of the faith have been produced. There have also arisen—and this is much more significant—a great many new confessions of faith,[42] which from the point of view of content and language cannot always be distinguished from theological short-formulas. These new confessions have arisen in Protestant and Catholic churches, and in young churches in all continents. They have arisen in base communities, in crisis situations, or in newly developing churches. Many of these confessions have a critically renewing interest.

None of these confessions, however, seeks to correct the creeds which belong to the whole Christian Church. Many adopt the trinitarian structure, or the triad of creation, redemption and reconciliation. But in almost all of them are reflected particular experiences of suffering and hope, and the mission to create a more human world. In unexpected language or metaphor, there may be more direct statements about what these Christians experience as their own faith. These do not, however, give the impression of a Babel-like confusion of language, but rather the fascinating richness of languages complementing each other in confession of the one God and Father of Jesus Christ. Pentecost, as the miracle of the many languages brought together in harmony, is a reality largely unnoticed by the Church's teaching office. Theologically different, and in theological terms often unreconciled, statements come to be reconciled in a common praxis. Orthodoxy in the traditional sense, where praxis is neglected, has only a relative value as a yard-stick for assessing such statements.[43] Even the teaching office of the Church has only a subsidiary function. In short, the unity of these Christian confessions is not directed from above, but it grows out of a renewed consciousness of following Jesus and of expectation of the Kingdom of God.

(c) No monoculture

The same is true of theologically developed short-formulas or summaries of the Christian faith. In theological terms they mirror a cultural, political and social variety of theological reflection which was not and could not be repressed. Overall, however, at a critical time in Catholic theology, they have sharpened one's vision for the discerning of spirits, and to a considerable degree have structured dialogue about the faith in a non-Christian world. Thus they have become, since the Council, important mileposts on the way to working out a communicable logical basis for the Christian faith. The undertaking has also shown, however, that this logical basis cannot be achieved without a hermeneutic of social praxis.

What can we learn from this for the project of a 'world catechism'? Simply this: that the world catechism—if it is to be achieved at all—must be the last stage in a multiplicity of experiments in which the churches come to an understanding, in the context of their respective cultures and traditions, of their practice and their witness, on the basic statements of the Christian faith. That means, however: the churches of different lands, cultures and continents would need first to come to an understanding themselves on their own plurality and polarity. They would need first to learn how to deal fruitfully with their own contradictions and conflicts in such a way that a brotherly, practical and theoretical system of communication might be built up. Initiatives 'from above' necessarily lose the experience and praxis within which alone the interpretation of the faith can be clear and liberating.

On the basis of experiences with short-formulas of the faith (these catechisms in the shortest form), is a world catechism at all desirable? Somewhat polemically, J. Ratzinger refers, in the context of short-formulas, to the 'oldest catechetical tradition', in which (as later with Luther) the Decalogue, the Lord's Prayer, the sacraments and the creed are expounded. 'I frankly find it hard to understand why today we are no longer capable of this restraint, but feel obliged to compile even school books on the basis of highly refined thought systems.'[44] This thought is worth taking up, in view of the proposal for a world catechism. In fact it does not make sense to impose the monoculture of a single theological system on the world Church. Decalogue, Lord's Prayer, sacraments and creed are in fact sufficient as binding elements on all, as elements safeguarding the common faith of all. A world church should be capable of such restraint. If these elements are interpreted on the basis of the experience of Jesus and applied to present-day experience, and if they are being constantly understood afresh, they are more than enough for unity and peace.

Translated by G. W. S. Knowles

Notes

1. 'Kurzer Inbegriff des christlichen Glaubens für "Ungläubige"' in *Geist und Leben* 38 (1965), 374–379; 'Die Forderung nach einer "Kurzformel" des christlichen Glaubens' in *Concilium* 3 (1967), 202–207 = *Schriften zur Theologie* VIII (Einsiedeln 1967), pp. 153–164.

2. 'Reflexionen zur Problematik einer Kurzformel des Glaubens' in *Schriften zur Theologie* IX (Einsiedeln 1970), pp. 242–256; 'Kurzformeln des Glaubens' in *Grundkurs des Glaubens. Einführung in den Begriff des Christentums* (Freiburg 1976), pp. 430–440.

3. 'Was ist die christliche Botschaft?' in *Die Zukunft der Kirche. Berichtband des Concilium-Kongresses 1970* (Zürich/Mainz 1971), pp. 84f.

4. Th. Schneider, 'Kurzformeln des Glaubens. Zur Problematik der Reduktion theologischer Aussagen' in *Catholica* 25 (1971), 179–197.

5. H. Schuster, 'Kurzformeln des Glaubens und seiner Verkündigung' in E. Hesse, H. Erharter (eds.) *Rechenschaft vom Glauben* (Vienna 1969), pp. 117–135.

6. A. Stock, *Kurzformeln des Glaubens* (Zurich 1971).

7. R. Bleistein, *Kurzformel des Glaubens* (Würzburg 1971)—I Prinzip einer modernen Religionspadagogik; II Texte.

8. F. Mussner, 'Eine neutestamentliche Kurzformel für das Christentum' in *Trierer theologische Zeitschrift* 79 (1979), 49–52.

9. F. Varillon, 'Un abrégé de la foi catholique' in *Informations catholiques Internationales* Nr. 290 = in *Collection prière et vie* (Toulouse 1968).

10. J. Ratzinger, 'kurzformeln des Glaubens? Uber das Verhaltnis von Formel und Auslegung' in J. Ratzinger *Theologische Prinzipienlehre. Bausteine zur Fundamentaltheologie* (Munich 1982), pp. 127–139; followed by 'Kurzformeln des Glaubens' in *Intern. kath. Zeitschr. Communio* 2 (1973), 258–263.

11. K. Lehmann, 'Bedarf das Glaubensbekenntnis einer Neufassung?' in P. Brunner *et al., Veraltetes Glaubensbekenntnis? Cf.* K. Lehmann, *Auferweckt am dritten Tag nach der Schrift* (Freiburg 1968; Regensburg 1968), pp. 125–168; and 'Kurzformeln des christlichen Glaubens' in B. Dreher *et al.*, (eds.), *Handbuch der Verkundigung I* (Freiburg 1970), pp. 274–295.

12. *AAS* 60 (1968), 433–445.

13. 'Dokumentation Concilium: Unruhe um das Glaubensbekenntnis' in *Concilium* 6 (1970), 63–74.

14. L. Karrer, *Der Glaube in Kurzformeln. Zur theologischen und sprachtheoretischen Problematik und zur religionspadagogischen Verwendung der Kurzformeln des Glaubens* (Mainz 1978). In this publication all the relevant literature is listed.

15. J. Ratzinger, *loc. cit.*, p. 128. This passage can be regarded as a typical example of an unfair and hostile interpretation.

16. K. Rahner (1970). K. Lehmann also lays emphasis on this point (1970), p. 275.

17. K. Rahner (1970), pp. 154f.

18. K. Rahner 'Reflexionen', p. 242.

19. This impulse received official confirmation in the doctrine of the 'hierarchy

of truths' (*Unitatis redintegratio* 11), but from the Roman side it has been interpreted in a restricted sense. For the history of its origin and operation see H. Witte, *Alnaargelang hun band met het fundament van het christelijk geloof verschillend is. Wording en verwerking van de uitspraak over de 'hiërarchie' van waarheden van Vaticanum II* (2 vols.) (Tilburg 1986); A. Houtepen '*Hierarchia Veritatum* and Orthodoxy' in *Concilium* 192 (Edinburgh 1987), 39–52.

20. L. Karrer, *loc. cit.*, pp. 235–244. Karrer takes as the basis of religious instruction very short formulas which not only indicate the essence of Christian belief, but also the profound basic structures of human life, with the question of its meaning, drawn from 'frontier experiences'. This provides a boundary for the discussion: the short-formula becomes a slogan or rallying-call, a 'contact-formula', which does not present a ready-made answer but starts off a process of communication. Behind this development lies the recognition that faith can only be 'concretely' expressed, claimed and put into practice in concrete situations. Otherwise it will shrivel away in dead husks of words.

21. *E.g.*: Ps. 114:1f.; Exod. 20:2; Deut. 6:20–25 (Lehmann, *kurzformeln*, pp. 278–282).

22. Mussner, *loc. cit.*, p. 49; see Karrer, *loc. cit.*, p. 28.

23. Mussner's own formula, as he says with reference to K. Rahner, is 'first biblical, and secondly develops not in a philosophical/transcendental way from man's self-understanding, but in a concrete way from his activity, since in the biblical understanding love always means activity' (Mussner, *loc. cit.*, p. 51).

24. H. Küng, *loc. cit.*, p. 78; and *Christ sein* (Munich 1974), p. 594 [ET *On Being A Christian* (London 1978), p. 602].

25. We may recall publications on theology, christology, ecclesiology, soteriology, and basic theological questions by, among others, K. Rahner, Y. Congar, E. Schillebeeckx, H. Küng, J. B. Metz—to mention only European writers.

26. F. Mussner, *loc. cit.*

27. K. Rahner's first formula runs as follows: 'The uncontainable whither and wherefore of human transcendence, which comes about existentially and primitively—not only theoretically or conceptually—is called God, and imparts itself existentially and historically to men, as their own perfection in forgiving love. The eschatological climax of the historical self-communication of God, in which this self-communication is revealed as irreversibly victorious, is called Jesus Christ' (*Grunkurs*, pp. 437f.).

28. The main formula runs: 'By following Jesus Christ man in the world of today can truly humanly live, act, suffer and die: in happiness and unhappiness, life and death, sustained by God and helpful to men' (*Christ sein*, p. 594 = *On Being A Christian*, p. 602).

29. *Die Zukunft der Kirche. Berichtband* (see n. 3).

30. 'Not to have permitted this open dialogue would have been a sign of mistrust of the inwardly convincing power of truth, as though it needed to be safeguarded by all possible kinds of disciplinary and inquisitorial measures' (W. Kasper, 'Die Funktion der Theologie in der Kirche' in *Die Zukunft der Kirche*, pp. 45–52).

31. R. Brown, as an exegete, refers to God, who acts in Jesus Christ; to Jesus Christ who was handed over to death and raised from death; to the words and deeds of Jesus, and to the fellowship of believers, by whom the message is passed on. K. Rahner deepens the fundamental theological, christological and ecclesial dimension of the answer. H. Küng breaks through the constraints of modern theology by placing the earthly and risen Jesus at the centre of his report (*Die Zukunft der Kirche*, 68–85).

32. *loc. cit.*, pp. 86–117.

33. J.-P. Jossua, 'Von der Theologie zum Theologen' in *Die Zukunft der Kirche*, pp. 53–59.

34. G. Baum, 'Die Präsenz der Kirche in der Gesellschaft von morgen' in *Die Zukunft der Kirche*, pp. 97–105.

35. J. B. Metz, 'Zur Präsenz der Kirche in der Gesellschaft' in *Die Zukunft der Kirche*, pp. 86–96.

36. Additional resolutions 2–5 in *Die Zukunft der Kirche*, pp. 153f.

37. K. Rahner (*loc. cit.*, 1970) had already called attention to this. As a result, the periodical *Concilium*, in early 1971, under the motto of a 'new image', subjected its organisation and programme to a thorough revision (H. Häring, 'Eine der meistzitierten Zeitschriften' in *Börsenblatt für den deutschen Buchhandel* 16, pp. 596–599).

38. J. Ratzinger reflects four kinds of symbols: the baptismal symbol, the conciliar symbol, the ordination symbol, and the kind of confession represented by the Confessio Augustana.

39. J. Ratzinger, *loc. cit.*, p. 135.

40. The simplistic distinction was made possible by the inappropriately objective category of 'facts of the faith', which Ratzinger himself has elsewhere revised.

41. Quotations from *loc. cit.*, pp. 131–137.

42. G. Goeters *et al.*, (eds.), *Bekenntnisse der Kirche. Bekenntnistexte aus zwanzig Jahrhunderten* (Wuppertal 1970); K. Lehmann, *loc. cit.*, pp. 283–286; P. Hoogeven (ed.) *Belijden in context: I. 37 nieuwere geloofsbelijdenissen 1963–1980; II. Tendenzen en motieven in het actuele christelijke belijden* (Leiden/Utrecht 1985). See further the WCC Faith and Order series, begun in 1980: *Confessing our Faith around the World*.

43. T. R. Peters, 'Orthodoxy in the Dialectic of Theory and Practice', *Concilium* 192 (Edinburgh 1987), 73–83.

44. J. Ratzinger, *loc. cit.*, p. 136.

PART III

World Catechism versus Inculturation?

Johann-Baptist Metz

Unity and Diversity: Problems and Prospects for Inculturation

1. The new situation in the Church's history

PEOPLE RIGHTLY talk today about a new phase in the history of the Church. After what was in time a relatively short period, but one which was fundamental to theological and historical identity of the Church, namely that of Judaeo-Christianity, the Church was dominated for almost 2,000 years by a relatively uniform cultural sphere, that of Europe and the West. Now the Catholic Church stands before a break in its history, one which in my view must been seen as the most far-reaching since the time of the primitive Church. The Church is in the process of moving from being a culturally more or less uniform, that is, a culturally monocentric, European (and North American) church to becoming a world church with a diversity of cultural roots and so in this sense, polycentric.[1] The last Vatican Council can be seen as a tangible institutional expression of this.[2]

This situation confronts the Church in a totally new and dramatic form with the problem of 'unity and diversity'. This issue lies at the heart both of the planned 'universal catechism' and of the discussion about the meaning and scope of what is called (inculturation', which this article will discuss in detail. What will be crucial to the handling of this new situation is whether this dramatic tension between unity and diversity is met by purely defensive safety-first mentality or whether an offensive loyalty to the Church's mission ultimately prevails, something like what Karl Rahner called 'prudent risk-taking'.

79

79

2. Problems of a polycentric inculturation

In this section I would like to concentrate on two difficulties created by the bold move to a polycentric world church.

The first difficulty has to do with the situation of our present-day world, and the global processes and tendencies visible in it. Talk of a culturally polycentric world church presupposes that real cultural polycentrism exists in today's world. However, this is far less obvious than it may appear at first sight. It seems to me increasingly hard to avoid asking whether macro-cultural diversity in our world is not gradually disappearing; is not, slowly but surely, being broken down or absorbed by the secular Europeanisation of the whole world which we call 'science' and 'technology' or 'technological civilisation'. This Western rationality increasingly rings the world with its technology and its culture and information industry, and it changes, not just the way people act, but clearly also the way they think. It is as though non-European peoples and cultures were being pulled into a 'Eurocentric whirlpool'.

> What makes one's heart sink is not the fact that the population of a poor country should press, with gentle but elemental force, for an improvement in their living conditions, but the process of compulsory imitation which this sets off . . . The stereotype of progress is increasingly questioned by Europeans and North Americans; it reigns unchallenged now only in the 'developing countries' of Asia, Africa and Latin America. Other people are the real Eurocentrics.[3]

Even if such language may be thought exaggerated, it can hardly be denied that non-Western peoples and cultures have already come under intense pressure to conform to the secular Europeanisation of the world. This fact raises the question whether cultural polycentrism in our world is not already rotten at the core. Is there really enough cultural identity and resistance left to fight this worldwide movement of European civilisation, which diffuses its myths of progress as well as its undeniable advances? It is not just theologians today who are worried by the question of how ethnic and cultural diversification in our world, that is, its cultural polycentrism, can be preserved in the face of a uniform world civilisation with no substance.[4]

If we reply by suggesting that there still exists a living and resistant cultural polycentrism, this brings us to the real theological question, and our second difficulty. If this is the case, how does the Church, in the process of becoming a real world church, connect with these non-European cultures if it clearly cannot treat the plans of a universal technological civilisation, the secular Europeanisation of the world, as an innocent vehicle for the universal propagation of its message? As is well known, this central question is dealt with in current theological discussion under the heading of 'inculturation'. I cannot here go into all the implications of this concept as it is used in the Church and in theology, but I am anxious to remove in advance one misunderstanding which is very frequently associated with the idea of the implantation of Christianity in non-Western countries. It is impossible not to mention this misunderstanding, even though doing so makes the problem of inculturation more difficult rather than easier.

Many well-meaning attempts are made these days to preserve the Church from ethnocentric fallacies and, for the sake of cultural polycentrism, to prevent a second seizure of power in the universal Church by Europe. These attempts are often accompanied by suggestions such as these: Christianity must at last remove its European garb, strip off its European and Western skin, and so on. What evidently underlies this language is the idea of an historical Christianity, a Christianity distinct from culture and innocent of ethnic ties. Another way of putting this is to say that the underlying idea is that of a 'pure' or 'naked' Christianity, which begins with nothing but itself and only clothes itself in the garments of different cultures in a subsequent act, when it already has its fixed identity, distinct from culture and history. This idea is a fiction; it feeds on unexamined metaphorical talk about naked facts of 'pure truth'. There is no such thing as a Christianity existing prior to culture and history, culturally free or naked Christianity. That is why the constantly implied parallel between inculturation and incarnation is only partially correct. Even the distinction which has grown up within (*sic*) European Christianity between religion and culture does not get us much further here, since it too is a culturally specific formulation.

The culture which ecclesial Christianity cannot simply take off like a garment is the European and Western culture formed from Jewish and Hellenistic Greek traditions. With regard to inculturation this raises the explosive question: if the Church cannot just strip off this historically contingent clothing and slip into some other new cultural garb, how can there ever be such a thing as a culturally polycentric world church? On these assumptions how can there be an inculturation of the gospel which is not Western expansion merely disguised for tactical reasons? In other words, is what we call cultural polycentrism in the last resort anything other than the continuation of a monocultural colonisation of the souls of foreign peoples and cultures by less drastic means than in previous epochs of church history?

This brings out the whole explosive and dramatic nature of the issue of 'unity and diversity' in the present ecclesiastical and ecumenical situation. It contains within itself a variety of dangers: the danger of an intensified official centralism as a defensive protection for unity, the speculative danger of a gnosis remote from history offered as a transcendental basis for the culturally polycentric diversity of Christianity, and the associated danger that the fixed and unchangeable 'deposit' of doctrinal and moral teaching will be envisaged as like Plato's ideas,[5] and the parallel 'liberal' danger of envisaging cultural polycentrism as a neutral and innocent coexistence of cultural contexts.

3. Conditions for a successful polycentrism

To the questions outlined above I would like to offer the following tentative answer as a starting-point for discussion. A culturally polycentric world church, which nevertheless must not and cannot step out of its Western European history, is possible on condition that, within the domain of European culture, this church remembers and acts on two basic features of its biblical inheritance. First, it must see itself as, and prove itself, in terms of its biblical inheritance, to be a religion committed by its mission to seeking freedom and justice for all. Second, it must see itself as and prove itself to be a religion which derives from its biblical inheritance a particular culture, a culture based on the acknowledgment of the other in their otherness, in other words on the creative acknowledgment of ethnic and cultural plurality, such as ought to be familiar to us from the primitive history of Christianity.

The two basic principles are indivisible. Nevertheless in this article I do not wish to devote any more attention to the question how far the Church must translate the biblical inheritance into the basis of a political culture which seeks freedom and justice for all. Discussion about political theology and the theology of liberation had made important advances here in recent years. My main concern here is to stress that a church which is maturing into a universal cultural polycentrism must treat and implement the biblical inheritance primarily as the basis of a hermeneutical culture, that is a culture which acknowledges the other in their otherness. This is particularly important because the European mentality as formed over the last 2,000 years, while it has internalised the biblical universalism whose limit is the 'ends of the earth' (see Acts 1:8), has been guided in this far more by the principle of domination than by that of acknowledgment. In his book *Die Eroberung Amerikas. Das Problem des Anderen*,[6] T. Todorov shows that this conquest succeeded because the Europeans were superior to the indigenous peoples in hermeneutics. While, for example, the Aztec could only understand and locate Cortes' tiny group within their own 'world picture', and therefore evaluated it wrongly, the Europeans were in a position to understand, evaluate and outwit these alien others in their otherness, almost in terms of their own 'system'. However, this understanding of others in their otherness was, as we know, no acknowledgment: it was primarily the expression of a hermeneutics of domination, not of a hermeneutics of acknowledgment.

In Christianity's biblical origins the encounter with strangers and the acknowledgment of others in their otherness was central. The welcoming approach to strangers who are different from oneself is a fundamental biblical attitude, which is constantly remarked on in the stories about Jesus. And many of Jesus' parables point to the dimension of promise present in the acknowledgment of the other, the one who is different. In other words, the origins of Christianity contain the seeds of a hermeneutical culture based on acknowledgment, which in the history of Europe was grossly obscured and fell into the background, and has never in the course of church history won that universal significance that might have been expected from its biblical origins. The Church seems constantly to have fallen victim to the temptation to confuse it's own universalism, the universality given to it with its mission, with the universality of the kingdom of God, and to neglect or ignore the eschatological difference between the Church and the kingdom of God.

The last Vatican Council is a prime example of moves towards a culture promoted by the Church itself which is based on the acknowledgment of the other in their otherness. In the declaration on the relationship of the Church to non-Christian religions the previous purely apologetic and defensive attitude to these religions and their cultures was for the first time replaced by a recommendation to see them in a positive light, even though it would have been good to have more detailed guidance about whether and how far the Church itself has to listen to the alien prophecy of these religions. In the degree on religious freedom the Church defines itself as the institutionalisation of a religion of freedom, which in the proclamation and propagation of its convictions rejects any means of coercion which circumvent that freedom. It does so because it seeks to be guided, not by an abstract right of truth, but by the right of the (other) person in their truth.

In language which is today familiar both in theology and in the Church at large, we might say that the Church must develop two options in order to meet the challenge of cultural polycentrism without denying its own cultural background. It must let itself be led by an option for the poor and an option for others in their otherness. It must translate this culture into practice in a political culture of freedom and complete justice and in a hermeneutical culture based on the acknowledgment of others in their otherness; and it must keep in mind all the time the link between these two options. This leaves us not only with many social barriers to overcome, but also much ethnic blindness in our traditional Christianity and the ethnic deficit of traditional Christian anthropology. The two options are often seen as two sides of a coin, but in my opinion ethnic and cultural diversity and social class differences cannot be simply identified. Ethnic and cultural particularities are not just an ideological superstructure generated by underlying economic problems, as both Western practice and Marxist theory might imply.

A culture based on the acknowledgment of others in their otherness, rooted in Judaism and Christianity but not seeking world unity by conquering others who are alien or weak and forcing them to pay the price for our European progress, would make it possible for the tendency to universality which has become a part of the European outlook to combine with the wisdom and sufferings of other cultures as promise. A coalition seems to me completely possible between two elements. Non-European cultures have resisted the abstract European logic of evolution in which history is finally replaced by natural economic laws and memory by computers. The European partners would be those who are also searching today—not seeking to abolish our scientific and technological world and its achievements, but certainly looking for new ways of interacting with that world. They are aware of the cultural background of our technological rationality and its increasingly automatic and anonymous processes of modernisation, in which human beings are less and less their own memories and more and more their own guinea-pigs.[7]

Unless I am making a mistake, one of the main obstacles to the development of a culture of acknowledgment in Church and theology is the predominance of an epistemological principle which entered Christianity through Plotinus. I mean the epistemological principle according to which like is always known by like. If we follow the biblical traditions, if we follow Paul (for example, in his conflict with Peter), we must formulate a different principle of knowledge for the Church and theology, one which states that only unlike can know unlike—in mutual acknowledgment. This remark leads to the next stage in our discussion.

4. Tasks for theology

The process of developing cultural polycentrism in the Church confronts theology with new tasks. First we must realise that the concept of theology current in the Church and the distinction it presupposes between theology and the living of religion is itself culture-specific and marked by ethnocentricity: this concept of theology itself derives from European and Western tradition. This must be firmly realised before we talk today about non-European theologies. If traditional theology is to take account of the conditions and assumptions under which the Church is maturing into cultural polycentrism, then it must on its side attempt to develop what I would tentatively call bridging categories in intercultural exchange.

One such category for promising intercultural mediation is, it seems to me, that of memory, and especially in the form of remembering suffering. The Church, of course, from its beginnings, is a remembering and retelling community gathered around the eucharist to devote itself to following Jesus. This characteristic gives it potential for intercultural communication and inculturation. I would propose the hypothesis, which I believe could be firmed up with empirical evidence, that memory and retelling should be regarded as more valuable for productive interchange between different cultures than the anonymous argumentation of classical metaphysics or the scientific language of Western rationality, which must both be regarded as specifically Eurocentric: indeed Western rationality cannot lead to cultural polycentrism, but only to an acceleration of the secular Europeanisation of the world through technology and the culture industry.

If this is correct, it is the task of theology today to protect remembering and retelling from suspicion of reductionism and homogenisation and to develop their communicative value, indeed superiority, for intercultural exchange. It is true that the category of remembrance and the associated basic anamnetic structure of Christianity are not exactly the focal point of theological attention at present. Indeed, Christian theology's reasoning has difficulty in coming to terms with this category. Under the influence of the categories of classical Greek idealist metaphysics remembrance has been split off from theological reasoning: memory appears only in the liturgy, and is regarded as primarily a part of worship and not strictly belonging to theo-logy or thinking about God. In my view this exclusion of the basic anamnetic structure of Christianity is connected with the fact that very early in the history of Christianity something like an attack of schizophrenia occurred. More and more the view gained ground in Christian theology that, while the faith of Christians might have its roots in Israel, their ideas derived—exclusively—from Athens, from Hellenism. While it would be wrong to minimise or underestimate the importance of Greek ideas for Christianity, there remains a question to be faced which is particularly urgent today: has Israel on its own no intellectual contribution to make to Christianity and Europe? Indeed it has, and Israel's intellectual and rational contribution to Christianity is an original one. It is the conception of thought as remembering, as historical remembrance, as that memory which is of crucial importance especially in intercultural exchange. This is something I feel must be taken very seriously in present-day theology with an eye to the beginnings of polycentrism.[8]

In the face of this new situation in church history theology is left with an important hermeneutical task in the interpretation of dogma. While the dogmas of the faith have been formulated with an over-reliance on Greek metaphysics, the need is not to dilute them, and certainly not to deny them; but there is a need to try to make them intelligible and to decode them as formulations of a dangerous memory,[9] as abbreviated formulas, shorthand 'dangerous stories' in which the substance of the faith can be communicated between cultures.

There are of course many dimensions to the claim of memory to be a privileged category of intercultural exchange. For the indigenous peoples of Latin America, for example, land and the soil is not simply a potential means of production, but the living space of their collective memory, the locus of their history. When this soil is taken from them, this land stolen, their memory is destroyed, and with it the organ they need to be genuinely evangelised. The current campaign of the Brazilian bishops against such land theft is therefore an example of a battle for a non-colonialist evangelisation.[10]

This brings our discussion into the sphere of ecclesiology and pastoral theology. The main question for theology here is who are the agents of a polycentric inculturation. Guided by the suggestions of the last Council, theology here must develop and establish the idea that the regional particular churches and the local churches must be given an important role in the development of a successful inculturation, and that the authority and responsibility of believers stressed by the Council, that is, their participation in the life of the Church in their own right is of crucial importance to the process of polycentric inculturation. This, however, opens another chapter of this discussion.

Translated by Francis McDonagh

Notes

1 On this see the relevant essays of mine in: Franz-Xaver Kaufmann and Johann-Baptist Metz, *Zukunftsfahigkeit. Suchbewegungen im Christentum* (1987).
2 On the signs and Vatican II statements which point in this direction see, in addition to the texts cited in note 1 above, Karl Rahner's essays in his *Schriften zur Theologie* XIV (1980).

3 Hans Magnus Enzenzberger, 'Eurozentrismus wider Willen', in: Enzenzberger, *Politische Brosamen* (1982), pp. 40, 42.

4 On these issues see also the article by Peter Rottländer in this issue.

5 For a criticism of this approach see Herbert Vorgrimler, 'The Adventure of a New "World Catechism"', *Concilium* 192 (Edinburgh 1987), 103–109.

6 French edition 1982, German 1985.

7 The hermeneutical culture of acknowledgment sketched out here is not just important for the new situation of the Church on the road to cultural polycentrism; it is also important for the situation of our world as a whole. Only if such a culture of acknowledgment becomes established can the emerging 'one world' become something other than the expression of an undifferentiated and empty or a repressive uniform world civilisation.

8 This aspect reveals the ecumenical significance of this new, culturally polycentric phase of church history. On the one hand in the perspective of a culturally polycentric world church the sixteenth-century split in the Church appears as primarily an internal European event. This does not make it less important, but gives it a new place among the new priorities of the ecumenical consciousness: the gradual superseding of a narrow, Eurocentric image of the Church may indirectly bring the histories of the European churches closer together and lead them to a new unity. On the other hand one important—and long overdue—result of the move towards a culturally polycentric world church may be to bring about a more productive ecumenical relationship between Christians and Jews, between Church and synagogue. In practice the European Gentile Christianity which grew up on Hellenistic soil was too heavily marked and defined by a contrast with its Jewish origins, and this is one of the reasons why antisemitism has lain so near the surface for most of past church history. If particular churches now work through their distinctive cultural identities to rediscover their origin and common past, the fundamental Jewish component will become clearer.

9 On this see my thoughts in J.-B. Metz, *Faith in History and Society* (London 1980).

10 On this see Alberto Moreira, 'Orthodoxy for the Protection of the Poor?', *Concilium* 192 (Edinburgh 1987), 110–115.

Emilio Alberich

Is the Universal Catechism an Obstacle or a Catalyst in the Process of Inculturation?

1. Catechisms and inculturation; a look at the past

THE ORIGINS and the diffusion of catechisms in the course of recent history have coincided to a certain extent with a new and decisive phase in the history of the inculturation of the Christian faith, and an important element in this process has been the development of missions outside Europe; the Portuguese and the Spanish have been particularly active in this sphere both in Asia and in America since the sixteenth century. Contacts between Christianity and other cultures and traditions which were so different from those of Europe soon began to create serious difficulties regarding the adaptation or the interpretation of the Christian faith in terms of the cultural limits of other peoples. Eloquent testimonies abound of the sensitivity of both missionaries and their home churches in attempting to find an adequate solution to the problem.[1]

In regard to this particular aspect of evangelisation, the specific function fulfilled by catechisms can surely be investigated. From the sixteenth century onwards, there is no lack of telling evidence of the efforts of missionaries both in Asia and in America to put together new catechisms intended for specific linguistic and cultural groups; but, a contrary movement towards uniformity quickly gained ground. Even as early as 1626 and within four years of its foundation, the Congregation for the Propagation of the Faith had established a polyglot printing press with the defined aim of publishing religious books in different languages, including catechisms. And, in regard to the latter, the commonest texts were the *Roman Catechism ad parochos* and Cardinal Bellarmine's *Christian Doctrine* which was imposed on different parts of Asia as early as 1632.[2]

In fact, even within this first phase in the history of catechisms the relationship between the desire for uniformity and the new awareness of the need for inculturation ought to be investigated. A general and, of necessity, schematic over-view brings to light a very negative result. For instance, the imposition of the Bellarmine catechism in Asia made a significant contribution to crystalising the cultural foreignness of Christians in that continent: 'This *ahistoric* catechism spread rapidly throughout Asia and contributed towards the creation of both psychological and social ghettoes of Christian communities in the continent. From then onwards, catechisms tended to be literal translations of texts which had been created for other cultural milieux.'[3]

In reference to their own particular and individual situations, the bishops of Africa expressed similar opinions at the time of the 1974 Synod.[4]

It is an acknowledged fact that the desire to standardise catechisms at regional, national and, latterly, at world levels has been growing increasingly in recent times but especially in the course of the last two hundred years. The First Vatican Council represents a very important stage in the process towards a universal catechism because such a project was on its agenda and the publication of such a catechism was approved. Despite the fact that the project never materialised, the idea was floated again on more than one occasion during the first few decades of this century to be eventually, and quite definitively, rejected by Vatican II[5] and by the Synod of 1977. Throughout this process from initial support to eventual abandonment of the idea of a universal catechism, the argument that favoured inculturation carried the day; and this was the case even when the cultural homogeneity demanded for *Christianity* did not favour *inculturation* to any extent. It could be argued that the extent to which the need for a real inculturation of the Christian faith is felt is also the measure of the extent to which the implantation of a universal catechism is considered as a possible obstacle to that need. Even at the First Vatican Council, Cardinal Rauscher, the Archbishop of Vienna, made that very point quite forcibly when he stated 'The attentive chorus of our enemies could shout out; "Here they are giving the very same catechism to Germans and to Indians; Oh, what sublime ignorance of the art of teaching!" '[6]

The same kind of arguments were presented regarding the very same issue at Vatican II: 'It does not seem to be in any way convenient that one catechism should be created for use in the universal Church, because there are far too many differences of culture and education amongst so many nations and peoples.'[7]

Accordingly, an over-view of the history of catechisms in recent times allows for an understanding of how they have almost always appeared so conditioned by the concrete, historical and cultural milieux that brought them to light, that they inevitably turned out to be quite useless in terms of their claims of universal and perennial relevance.[8] In the course of the last two hundred years, there has been a clear desire to produce one catechism which would be complete in itself and of value to everyone at local, national and universal levels. But, in reality, the partial successes achieved in this respect have never delayed the spread of local catechisms in all places and experience has shown that the attempt to create a universal catechism has generally exacerbated the difficulties of reconciling the demands of theology and of pedagogic catechesis.[9] The theological necessity of integrity and orthodoxy is at odds with the need to respect the recipients of the teaching, to adapt itself to their educational capacities and to ensure a meaningful transmission of the Christian message. On this particular point, time and again critics voiced their disagreement as different catechisms came into use but they went unheeded or were considered as of little consequences.[10]

2. The inculturation of the faith and catechesis; some essential requirements

Both the notion and the concept of *inculturation* have progressively advanced during the post-conciliar period; it was an underlying theme of the 1974 Synod which dealt with evangelisation, but it was brought right into the open in Paul VI's Apostolic Exhortation *Evangelii nuntiandi* (No. 20). Moreover, it is quite significant that it was at the 1977 Synod, which dealt with catechesis, that the topic was first properly mooted and that a definitive option was made for the term *inculturation*. The close connection between catechesis and inculturation was clearly expressed in the Synod's final statement:

As the second Ecumenical Council of the Vatican pointed out and as Paul VI recalled in the Apostolic Exhortaton *Evangelii nuntiandi*, the message of Christianity has to become rooted in all the different human cultures, embracing them and transforming them. Accordingly, it can be said that catechesis is at the service of *inculturation* which means that it serves to both develop and enlighten from within the lives of those to whom it is directed. (No. 5).

The same kind of statement is to be found in the exhortation of John Paul II, *Catechesi tradendae*:

Catechesis and evangelisation in general can be said to be directed at bringing the very essence of the Gospel into the very heart of culture itself and into all cultures. (No. 53).

Moreover, the present topic demands that the natural and close connection between inculturation and the reality of the *individual church* be given its proper emphasis. In this respect, what identifies the individual church in the light of *Evangelii nuntiandi* is its foundation and base within a specific cultural milieu:

Nevertheless this universal Church is in practice incarnate in the individual churches made up of such or such an actual part of mankind, speaking such and such a language, heirs of a cultural patrimony, of a vision of the world, of an historical past, of a particular human substratum. (No. 62).

According to this description, the individual church would constitute a reality which would itself extend beyond the narrow boundaries of the local church or diocese. And what has to be emphasised is the essential task which falls to these churches of being agents of inculturation, precisely because of their special relationship with the cultural reality that constitutes their specific character:

The individual churches, intimately built up not only of people but also of aspirations, of riches and limitations, of ways of praying, of loving, of looking at life and the world which distinguish this or that human gathering, have the task of assimilating the essence of the Gospel message and of transposing it, without the slightest betrayal of its essential truth, into the language that these particular people understand, then of proclaiming it in this language. (*Ibid.*, No. 63).

This task of inculturation has to be brought to completion in the liturgy, in theological reflection, in the ecclesial structures 'and in the areas of catechesis' (*ibid.*). Accordingly, the individual church, catechesis and culture would appear to be implicated in, and mutually interdependent within, the process of the inculturation of the faith. We can now consider some of the essential requirements of this process so that both the positive and negative outcomes engendered by any catechism may be better understood.

(a) Inculturation is a process of giving and receiving

The Synodal Message of 1977 stated: 'The real *incarnation* of the faith through catechesis involves not just the process of *giving* but also that of *receiving*. (No. 5). This means that not only must there be a process by which the faith transforms and purifies culture, but there also has to be a process by which the very faith itself has to be rethought and re-interpreted, naturally within clearly defined limits, and in the light of the categories and requirements of every culture. In this sense, cultures themselves must discharge the function of *hermeneutic criterion* in regard to the faith.

(b) Inculturation cannot be reduced to a mere adaptation of language

Inculturation is not simply a means of providing an external form for expressions of the contents of the faith which is seen as immutable and defined once and for all. Indeed, it is an acknowledged fact that the Christian faith does not exist in a pure state, isolated from cultural incarnations within historical milieux, since in every era and in every place it has to assume a vital contact with the categories, the ways of thinking and the existential demands proper to every culture. This requirement of cultural incarnation is a fundamental law of every effective form of evangelisation.

> With the help of the Holy Spirit, it is the task of the whole people of God, particularly of its pastors and theologians, to listen to and distinguish the many voices of our times and to interpret them in the light of the divine Word, in order that the revealed truth may be more deeply penetrated, better understood, and more suitably presented. *Gaudium et spes* (No. 44).

If, in the ordinary course of events and with particular reference to the inculturation of the faith, the problem of language is highlighted in view of the difficulties of providing a significant transmission of the Gospel message in every era, language itself, as *Evangelii nuntiandi* indicates,

> should be understood here less in the semantic or literary sense than in the sense which one may call anthropological and cultural. (No. 63).

Thus, the definitive aim is to achieve a true incarnation of the faith within the very core of each culture, so as to assume its values, its true aspirations and its particular standards:

Evangelisation loses much of its force and effectiveness if it does not take into consideration the actual people to whom it is addressed, if it does not use their language, their signs and symbols, if it does not answer the questions they ask, and if it does not have an impact on their concrete life. (*Ibid.*).

(c) Inculturation demands a balance between unity and pluralism within the Church

Despite what has already been said, the need to safeguard the identity and the unity of the Christian faith, both on the diachronic plane (fidelity to apostolicity) and on the synchronic plane (sense of catholicity), cannot be ignored. Genuine incarnation of the faith in different cultures can never be achieved at the expense of the loss of the catholic unity of that same faith:

Evangelisation risks losing its power and disappearing altogether if one empties or adulterates its content under the pretext of translating it; if, in other words, one sacrifices this reality and destroys the unity without which there is no universality. *Evangelii nuntiandi* (No. 63).

It is not difficult to discern the delicate balance that has to exist between adaptation to local needs and fidelity to the Christian identity, and between diversity and unity. In actual fact, these do not constitute opposing demands because an effective and proper incarnation of the faith in each culture will be more secure and better founded when its own awareness of universal communion is strong and certain:

The more an individual church is attached to the universal Church . . . the more such a church will be capable of translating the treasure of faith into the legitimate variety of expressions of the profession of faith, of prayer and worship, of Christian life and conduct and of the spiritual influence on the people among which it dwells. (*Ibid.*, No 64).

At the very heart of inculturation, therefore, there is a powerful need for fidelity to the immutable contents of the Christian faith, which must not be understood in terms of an external uniformity within a list of prefixed formulae, but rather in terms of an internal agreement with and communion with the very act of cultural incarnation itself.

While being translated into all expressions, this content must neither be impaired nor mutilated. While being clothed with the outward forms proper to each people, and made explicit by theological expression which takes account of differing cultural, social and even racial milieux, it must remain the content of the Catholic faith just exactly as the ecclesial Magisterium has received it and transmits it. (*Ibid.*, No. 65).

Accordingly, it is important that these criteria and essential requirements of the inculturation of the faith be kept in mind because they are recognised by the official documents of the *magisterium* of the Church, and because they underlie any response that could be made to the question posed at the very beginning of this article: *viz.*, will a universal catechism be an obstacle to the inculturation of the faith, or could it even, as a *catalyst*, benefit such a process?

3. A universal catechism and inculturation: possibilities and risks

It is not easy to forecast clearly whether the proposed universal catechism would have a positive or a negative effect on inculturation, because the effective spirit of its final edition is quite unknown and, what is even more important, there is no clear indication of the rôle it would carry in actual catechesis. At this point in time, there are many who have criticised the proposed compendium of doctrine and it is also important to point out that experts and researchers in catechetics have not received the proposal of a universal catechism with much enthusiasm.[11]

The above outline of the requirements of the process of inculturation raises serious doubts about the effectiveness of a catechism as a catalyst in such a process. Further complications arise from the development that has taken place, especially since the Council, in the practical concepts of catechism and catechesis. In the preconciliar tradition, catechisms appeared with fairly uniform and identifiable characteristics: they were generally seen as text books for the religious instruction of Christians and consisted of organic and systematic compendia of the Church's official teaching and were generally put together in terms of the categories and formulae of systematic theology. At the very core of this general concept it is easy to distinguish a pedagogic method and a clearly defined catechetical vision; a catechesis considered above all else as the magisterial transmission of the *fides quae*.

There has occurred in our day a radical change not just because of the cultural and religious co-ordination which has taken place in our era, but also because of the developments in pedagogic awareness and because of the new theological and pastoral concepts of Vatican II. In this way, the *era of the catechism* has come to an end; that is, if the phrase is understood as referring to a period in which catechesis was based on an exposition and understanding of the doctrinal compendium of the faith contained in the book commonly known as the catechism. Today, great emphasis is placed on the distinction between *catechism* and *catechesis*. The *catechism* should perhaps be a basic instrument or aid within the whole process of education in the faith but it has often exceeded this remit of simply transmitting religious knowledge.

Within this context, the post-conciliar catechisms have quite different functions according to the particular purpose for which they have been published and according to the catechetical context in which they are to be used. Some countries (*e.g.* France and Germany) have even opted for replacing the catechism by a continuous series of different catechetical aids, such as *compulsory resources*, reference books, work books and audio-visual aids, teaching projects, itineraries or *parcours*, anthologies of source documents of the faith, etc. On the other hand, other countries (*e.g.* The Netherlands, Italy and Spain) have opted for post-conciliar catechisms which constitute a real attempt at renovation and at the creation of a new catechetical approach. At all events, it would seem that, at the present time, a catechism has to be essentially different from what it was in the past and it will be necessary, therefore, to pay particular attention to each one in regard to content and aims so that a properly balanced judgment can be made. This distinction has also been admitted by those who are promoting a universal catechism and by those who have assumed responsibility for the project, which, as is well known, is not intended as a substitute for local catechisms but as a point of reference in the process of producing the latter.

It has to be acknowledged that even today, within certain limits, a catechism can be a worthwhile instrument at the service of achieving objectives of undoubted worth for the Christians of our own day and age. These objectives include, for example; facilitating a return to the very origins of the faith, rediscovering the essential elements of the Christian faith, achieving a complete and fully integrated vision of revealed truth, re-affirming the faith's own identity within the span of world-views and religious beliefs, etc.. Within that series of objectives, a catechism or a compendium of the faith could in itself make a significantly positive contribution to any process of inculturation which is properly undertaken.

However, history and experience teach us that we cannot forget the ever present risk of catechisms becoming real and, to a greater or lesser degree, deliberate instruments of standardisation and of an imposed uniformity; there is always the danger that individual theological positions are imposed as part of the essence of the faith or that matters which are essentially still open to further questioning and deeper understanding are deliberately presented as otherwise. Many catechisms still carry that hidden element which consists of the undeclared conviction that what is crucial in education in the faith is the exact transmission of contents which have been very clearly defined. The problem becomes particularly acute at the level of *language* and this occurs especially in reference to a *universal* catechism; in actual fact, it is practically impossible to present *in a properly connected series* expressions which are common to the faith without some real compromise of the requirement which has already been discussed in regard to formulating the Christian message:

> While being clothed with the outward forms proper to each people, and made explicit by theological expression which takes account of differing cultural, social and even racial milieux. *Evangelii nuntiandi* (No. 65).

A genuine and legitimate inculturation of the faith will be impossible if the future universal catechism sets out to establish one, unique language of faith, with the natural exception of the traditional patrimony of the sources, or attempts to create common doctrinal formulae which have to be learned by rote.

It would be quite a different scenario if the catechism did not just set out to clarify the living and essential nucleus of the Christian faith, but also deliberately undertook to provide a stimulus and a framework for the effective inculturation of the Christian message within different cultural milieux, effectively demonstrating the principle of the *hierarchy of truth* or even providing positive examples of areas in which aspects of the faith could be re-thought according to differing cultural contexts. In such a scenario, not only would it not be an obstacle but would be an effective incentive in the search for a meaningful and attractive proclamation of the Christian message to the world of today. The difficulties inherent in such an undertaking are obvious to everyone. However, within the context, it should perhaps have always been feasible to effect the suggestion which was made in 1983 by the International Council for Catechesis, with reference to the contemporary demands of evangelisation and catechesis, that the General Catechetical Directory published in 1971 by the Congregation for the Clergy should be re-modelled and up-dated.

Translated by John Angus Macdonald

Notes

1. *Cf.* the many references put together in the volume: Istituto di Catechesi Missionaria della Pontificia Università Urbaniana (ed.), *Andate e insegnate Commento all' Esortazione Apostolica* Catechesi Tradendae *di Giovanni Paolo II* (Bolonga 1980); and P. Borges, *Métodos misionales en la cristianización de América, Siglo XVI* (Madrid 1960).

2. *Cf.* J. Metzler, 'La catechesi missionaria nelle direttive della S. Congregazione per l' Evangelizzazione dei popoli o "De Propaganda Fide" (1633–1970), in *Istituto di Catechesi Missionaria, op. cit.*, pp. 704–706.

3. *Cf.* G. M. Zago, 'Catechesi in ambiente buddhista', in *Istituto di Catechesi Missionaria, op. cit.*, p. 569.

4. *Cf.* G. Butturini (ed.), *Le nuove vie del Vangelo* (Bologna 1975).

5. *Cf.* P. Palazzini, 'L' opera svolta dalla S. Congregazione per il Clero nel campo catechistico', in Sacra Congregazione per il Clero (ed.), *Atti del II Congresso Catechistica Internazionale, Roma 20–25 settembre, 1971*, (Rome 1972), pp. 204–206.

6. 'Vigilaus autem inimicorum cohors clamaret: ecce Germanis et Indis unum eundemque catechismum statuunt; o supina artis pedagogicae ignorantia': Mansi, *Sacrorum Conciliorum Nova et Amplissima Collectio*, Vol. 50 (Graz 1961), p. 709 B.

7. *Schemata Constitutionum et Decretorum ex quibus Argumenta in Concilio Disceptanda Seligentur*, Third Series (Rome 1962) p. 159; the original is in Latin.

8. *Cf.* A. García Suarez, 'Algunas reflexiones sobre el sentido y la evolución histórica de los catecismos en la Iglesia', *Actualidad Catequética*, No. 76 (1976) pp. 159–164; *Cf.* also, E. Alberich and U. Gianetto (eds.), *Il catechismo ieri e oggi*, 'Studi sul significato dei catechesmi nel passato e nel presente della catechesi della Chiesa' (Turin 1987).

9. *Cf.* E. Paul, 'Der Katechismus im Gesamt der Glaubensverkündigung' in E. Paul, G. Stachel and W. Langer, *Katechismus – Ja? Nein? Wie? Drei Diskussionsbeiträge* (Zurich/Einsiedeln/Cologne, 1982) pp. 26–27.

10. *Cf.* E. Paul, *loc. cit.*; *Cf.* also, L. Nordera, *Il catechismo di Pio X* (Rome 1988).

11. *Cf.* the recent Session of the European Catechetical Team, held in Gazzada, Italy, May 1988: and, E. Alberich, 'Verso il riconoscimento della competenza catechetica nella Chiesa', *Catechesi* 57 (1988), pp. 48–49.

Peter Schineller

Inculturation as the Pilgrimage to Catholicity

LIBERATION THEOLOGY in Latin America; the dialogue with the great religious traditions in Asia; inculturation of Christian faith in villages of Africa; ecumenical discussions between first world churches, the confrontation of Christianity with a technological, modernised society; the cry of women for equal opportunity in world and Church—each of these points to creativity and ferment present in Christian churches throughout the globe. Each movement contains positive possibilities for growth, a growth that is often painful. This growth continually calls into question the unity of the Church. As the Church moves into new dialogues and new contexts, how does it remain one, holy, catholic, and apostolic? In particular, two of the traditional four notes or marks of the Church come into question, namely oneness and catholicity. Oneness indicates unity, not uniformity, and catholicity points to the adaptability or openness of the Church to new contexts.[1] How does one understand, imagine, and live these two marks in such a way that they are mutually illuminating and increase together, so that the more catholic or universal the Church becomes, so much richer will be the unity?

1. Inculturation

The varied movements we sketched above can be viewed as examples of inculturation. The term may be new,[2] yet it points to the perennial challenge of living the gospel in one's particular time and place. A working definition of inculturation is 'the incarnation of Christian life and of the Christian message in a particular cultural context, in such a way that this experience not only finds expression through elements proper to the culture in question, but becomes a principle that animates, directs, and unifies the culture, transforming and remaking it so as to bring about a new creation' (*Arrupe*, 1978).

A brief description of the method of inculturation is also needed, for this will show why the process of inculturation raises the question of unity and catholicity.[3] Inculturation consists in putting the hermeneutical or pastoral circle into operation. This can be imagined as a circle with three poles, and with arrows pointing between the poles in both directions. The three poles represent (1) the cultural context or situation, (2) the Christian message, and (3) the pastoral agent or team. The pastoral agent or team is inserted or immersed in a situation with its problems and possibilities, values and disvalues. Then the agent, with his or her own particular gifts and strengths, brings that situation into dialogue and confrontation with the Christian message that confirms the good and challenges the evils of that situation.

Why the challenge to unity? Inculturation demands that much more attention than in traditional theology be given to the present, the novel, and the particular. The signs of the times are read, the voice of the spirit speaking today receives a full hearing. The complexity and the diversity of particular contexts is examined and celebrated as preparation for the interaction with the Christian message. At the same time, we are aware now of the complexity of the Christian message itself. There are four complementary gospels, and an almost 2,000 year history of the interpretation and living of those gospels. There is no one, uniform Christian tradition, but rather historically developing and diverse interpretations of the meaning of Jesus Christ for Christian life. Scripture and tradition are a vast and diverse treasure chest, rather than a solid block of gold. So too, the composition of the pastoral agent or team will make a difference in the outcome. A black woman in an African village will see God and God's world differently than a wealthy banker in New York or Hong Kong, or a bishop in Rome or Latin America. Each pastoral agent must bring his or her own experiences and talents to bear upon their way of inculturating gospel values in their context.

Put briefly, inculturation takes seriously the *who*, the *where*, the *with whom* and *for whom* one does theology and one builds church. In fact, the local community ideally should become the maker of theology, a theology that is in dialogue with the larger Church, but one that speaks God's word for that particular cultural situation. To do this, the key attitude needed in the process of inculturation is *listening*, listening to the word of God already present in seemingly secular contexts, the God who speaks to each Christian who shares in the prophetic office of Jesus Christ through baptism, the God who spoke above all in God's Son.

When such creativity is encouraged on the local level, whether that be a national bishops' conference, a diocese, a parish, or a base Christian community, there is the danger that this local group will lose its bonds with the larger Church and the larger tradition of the Church. In other words, by fostering catholicity through the process of inculturation—as recent Roman teaching has done—there is the danger of the breakdown of unity. Yet, as we will see, this need not be the case. In fact, the opposite should be true, namely that the process of inculturation is the only possible way to full catholicity. Part of the solution lies in how one conceives the unity of the Church. To that question we now turn.

2. Unity through complementarity

(a) Unity, not *uniformity*. Uniformity is stifling and uncreative. No living organism such as the Church can remain untouched, unaffected by the sweep of history, by the diversity of languages and cultures. Stress on uniformity, in fact, will lead to schism unless sufficient breathing space is allowed for local expression.

(b) Unity in *diversity*. If not uniformity, then what type of unity? Here we will examine two words that try to indicate such a unity, namely, diversity and pluralism. Diversity in its root meaning indicates one is turned in a different direction. But if one goes in a different direction, one's own way, then this can result in separation, disunity, or at worst, divisiveness. Thus this term is unstable and can be misunderstood.

(c) Unity and *pluralism*. In 1969, Pope Paul VI said that 'a certain pluralism is desirable'. But this cautious encouragement points to the ambiguity of the very word pluralism that cannot stand alone without qualification.[4] The International Theological Commission in 1972 tried to distinguish between true and false pluralism. We speak of a healthy or unhealthy pluralism. It seems therefore that the word pluralism must be qualified to be correctly understood. One way to move has been to speak of *pluriformity* as the Extraordinary Synod of Bishops did in 1985. 'It is necessary to distinguish pluriformity from pure pluralism. When pluriformity is true richness and carries with it fullness, this is true catholicity.' Yet even this move to pluriformity may not be able to free the word from its ambiguous interpretations.

(d) Unity through *complementarity*. Let me suggest this as the way to help in conceiving the shape of unity. Complementarity becomes the operative word, replacing diversity and pluralism, to point to full catholicity that is the result of the process of inculturation. The term is used in Vatican II in the decree on Ecumenism in the context of a discussion of the Churches of the East. There is a legitimate variety in understanding divine things, so that 'these various theological formulations are often to be considered as complementary rather than conflicting' (*Decree on Ecumenism*, No. 17).

What is the value of the language of complementarity? First, the root meaning *com/plere* means to fill out or to bring to fullness or completion. What is lacking in the whole is supplied in mutuality through the richness of the individuals. The riches of one makes up for the limitations of the other. Secondly, with its root of *cum* or *com*, it implies an ongoing relationship and communication among local churches, one with the other, and also with central leadership. To be complementary means to see oneself as part of a larger whole, yet also truly oneself, aware of one's particular gifts as well as limitations. A church that is truly complementary is never the lone individual, never simply going its own way but in dialogue and in solidarity with others. Thirdly, the words complement and compliment were originally the same. The meaning of compliment, namely to pay tribute, might be maintained as inherent in complementarity. That is, two churches that are in complementarity also compliment one another, or pay courtesy and give encouragement to each other. A local church in Africa, by being itself, is in fact contributing to the universal Church, both paying a compliment to the universal and receiving compliments from the universal. Fourthly, complementarity clearly rules out uniformity or an unhealthy pluralism. It implies that no one church can fully represent or be a sacrament of the whole Christ, or in other words, fully inculturate or incarnate the gospel in its ways and life. There must be interdependence to show forth the full, unfathomable richness of Christ. Fifthly, unity through complementarity reminds the Church that it is a pilgrim church on the road to fullness. As Vatican II expresses it, 'in virtue of this catholicity, each part contributes its own gifts to other parts and to the whole Church, so that the whole and each of the parts are strengthened by the common sharing of all things and by the common effort to attain to fullness in unity' (*Dogmatic Constitution on the Church*, No. 13). Full catholicity is ahead, in process of being realised. Sixthly, unity through complementarity indicates that we cannot think that at present we have an existing Catholic Church that has the fullness, and that inculturation is allowing diversity, or the centre encouraging the local churches to be local. This would lead us to believe that there is a finished standard against which other new churches are measured. Rather we should reverse the image and see that the full catholic unity is precisely in process of being built through the complementarity of the local churches.

Thus, by speaking of unity through complementarity rather than of uniformity, diversity, or pluralism we hope to indicate a possible image and path for the pilgrim Church. In this way will the equal dignity and rank of all Churches be preserved, as Vatican II insists (*Decree on the Catholic Eastern Churches*, No. 3). Each local church is viewed as having its unique challenge and task in building up the body of Christ.

3. Models of unity through complementarity

Instead of entering upon the important and difficult questions of the kernel or essence of the gospel that must be preserved at the local level, the distinction between the substantial and the accidental, the limits of diversity, the meaning and importance of the hierarchy of truths, and the possibility and limits of liturgical adaptation,[5] we will proceed by presenting examples or images of unity through complementarity, and then attitudes that are necessary for this to be achieved. These images are from the secular and the sacred realms, and function to help one envision a universal church that is on the road to the catholic fullness.

(a) A choir composed of men and women, old and young, where each sings his or her own best and yet blend together into harmony under the skilled director. In place of tiresome monotony and painful dissonance there is a rich unity through complementarity. So too, a symphony orchestra, or perhaps even better, a jazz band, with individual creativity and improvisation comes together into rich unity.

(b) The world of nature, diverse in colours and species, in variety of sounds and fragrances, yet one world or cosmos as seen so clearly by the astronauts from outer space.

(c) The rainbow or spectrum of colours that results from the refraction of sunlight. In fact, science speaks of complementary colours, meaning those two colours that together give a neutral colour of whitish grey.

(d) The United Nations, the Olympic Games, or a modern metropolis like New York City at their best. There we see the panoply of nations and races of the earth represented, living, sharing, playing, and working together to make up the family of humankind.

In the religious world, we also have constructive images of unity through complementarity.

(i) The four gospels, each in its own way, portraying, pointing creatively to the same Jesus Christ. No one of them would be sufficient, and even together they only begin to glimpse the fullness of Christ. The canon of scripture, rather than fostering uniformity, functions to recognise the validity of and mark the limits of acceptable diversity. It points to unity through complementarity.

(ii) Pauline theology of the body of Christ points to the one body, where the strong complement the weak, all parts working together to make up the body of Christ (Rom. 12:15ff., and 1 Cor. 12:12ff.). Related to that imagery is the theology of the charisms given to individual Christians which work together to form one Church (1 Cor. 12:4ff. and 1 Pet. 4:10ff.).

(iii) The beginning of the Church at Pentecost indicates how persons of different languages and cultures, can retain those languages and cultures, and come together in union through the one Spirit of Jesus Christ.

(iv) The variety of the communion of saints throughout Christian history. Men and women, old and young, African and European, bishops and catechumens, are affirmed as saints, and held forth as models, each in his or her own way pointing to a possible and complementary way of following Jesus Christ.

(v) The rich tradition of the Eastern Churches, together with the Western Churches that comprise Roman Catholicism. The Eastern Churches have preserved and developed their own institutions, liturgical rites and ordering of the Christian life. This in turn complements more western expressions, and enriches the universal Church. As Vatican II affirms, between Churches of the East and West 'there is a wonderful bond of union so that this variety in the Universal Church, so far from diminishing its unity, rather serves to emphasise it' (*Decree on the Catholic Eastern Churches*, No. 2).

In these models, and most concretely in the last model of the Catholic Eastern Churches, we have the possibility of envisioning a church whose catholicity and unity grow together, through the ongoing process of inculturation.

4. Strategies towards catholic unity

The key word we have explored is complementarity. But if catholic fullness and unity is to be achieved, then several other concepts, strategies, and attitudes must be operative at the local level as well as in the central Church authority. Each of the concepts represents a goal as well as a process and attitude that will lead to the goal of unity through complementarity. Each of the words involves the root *cum/com*, as does the word complementarity, indicating the pilgrimage that is made together, with other Christians to catholic fullness.

(a) *Communio*. Presuming that individual churches are in communion with God, Vatican II desires that churches enter into communion with different forms of culture, thereby enriching both themselves and the cultures (*Pastoral Constitution on the Church in the Modern World*, No. 58). So too the young churches must remain in intimate communion with the whole Church and thus, by a mutual outpouring of energy, increase the life of the mystical Body (*Decree on the Church's Missionary Activity*, No. 19).

(b) *Companion*. In its root meaning is to break and share bread together. Local churches must see themselves as companions on the journey, like the two disciples on the road to Emmaus. Related to companionship would be a synodal form of being church, since the root meaning of synod is to be 'together on the road'. No church can go its own way, but we move together, with the Eucharistic bread as strength and sign of unity for the journey.

(c) *Commissioned*. The first apostles were commissioned (Mt. 28), so the churches are today sent forth in mission, together. Individual churches must turn to and rely upon the resources and insights of other churches in carrying out the great commission. That commission today is further specified, with Luke 4, as the liberating mission to bring the gospel to the poor.

(d) *Collaborative*. All members of the Church, laity and clergy, must work together. Each has special gifts and responsibilities to bring to this task. Thus Vatican II: 'All the faithful have an obligation to collaborate in the expansion and spread of his Body, so that they might bring it to fullness as soon as possible' (*Decree on the Church's Missionary Activity*, No. 36).

(e) *Conversion*. All Christians and all local churches are involved in the ongoing and even deepening conversion to Jesus Christ. By moving closer to Jesus Christ, we are moving closer to each other. We do this together in complementarity.

(f) *Continuity*. Catholicity involves links across space and time. We are not isolated, but in continuity (literally, being held together) with churches of previous ages and present churches around the world today.

(g) *Communication*. Not isolation or silence, not one-way information, but mutual dialogue and communication among local churches and with the central authority will help assure that true catholicity is achieved through complementarity.

5. The path ahead

The inculturation which we speak of goes far beyond imposition, translation, or mere adaptation. With Vatican II we can speak of a more profound or radical adaptation whereby local traditions and the special qualities of each national family, illumined by the light of the gospel, are taken up into a catholic unity (*Decree on the Church's Missionary Activity*, No. 22). And here we face the gospel paradox of the two-edged sword. That is, the more radical the inculturation, the more freely and creatively that the local church interacts with its context, then the richer are the positive possibilities for fuller catholicity, but also the more danger of disunity or schism. Dulles has described catholicity as the holding together of opposites, and thus the more distant those opposites are, the more difficult it becomes to hold them together. But if they are held together as complementary, then a richer unity results.

There is no other way forward than to take this risk. Each local church must be encouraged to intensify its search to be truly local, truly Christian in its own time and place, but at the same time retain its links with both other local churches and the universal Church. The reason why this unity is within the range of possibility is because in trying to live the Christian life to the full in one's own circumstances, one will inevitably move into the paschal mystery of Jesus Christ. This mystery is the point where the truly human and the divine converge, where humanity of all cultures comes together on the journey. In fact, as Vatican II asserts, not only Christians, but all men and women are given this challenge of associating with the paschal mystery (*Pastoral Constitution on the Church in the Modern World*, No. 22). In this way, not only Christians, but all humanity moves together towards the fullness of Christ.

Jesus Christ is the one full of grace and truth, and of his fullness we have received (Jn. 1:14–16). As the grace and truth of Jesus Christ is a gift that involves a response, so is the catholicity of the Church a gift that involves a response, that of the ongoing effort at inculturation.

Some years ago, a veteran missioner described the shift that occurred in his image of himself as a missionary. Instead of being the one who brings the pearl of great price to the local church, he began to see himself as a treasure hunter, with the local people, for the grace and truth that was already with them, perhaps in hidden ways. Instead of one who had the questions and the answers, he saw himself as one engaged collaboratively in the search for the more full revelation of Jesus Christ, a process in which he would learn as well as share. This, I suggest, is a valid image for the universal Church in search of its true catholicity, the Church in the unending process of trying to fathom the unfathomable riches of Jesus Christ (Eph. 3:8).

Notes

1. For the meanings of catholicity, see Avery Dulles, *The Catholicity of the Church* (Oxford 1985).

2. On inculturation, the most helpful single volume would be Robert J. Schreiter, *Constructing Local Theologies* (New York/London 1985).

3. I have briefly developed ideas on the process of inculturation in 'Ten Summary Statements on the Meaning, Challenge, and Significance of Inculturation', in *On Being Church in a Modern Society* (Rome 1983); and 'The Role and Function of Jesus the Christ', in *Modern Biblical Scholarship: Its Impact on Theology and Proclamation* (Villanova, PA 1983).

4. David Tracy, *The Analogical Imagination* (New York/London 1981), as its subtitle—'Christian Theology and the Culture of Pluralism' indicates, explores the meaning of pluralism.

5. Two volumes that begin to explore these and related questions are *Concilium* 171 *Different Theologies, Common Responsibility: Bable or Pentecost?* (Edinburgh 1984) and *Concilium* 192 *Orthodoxy and Heterodoxy* (Edinburgh 1987).

Peter Rottländer

One World: Opportunity or Threat for the Global Church?

IN CURRENT theological discussion of questions dealing with the global Church, the two concepts 'one world' and 'inculturation' play an important role. Often, there is little regard for the fact that these two concepts designate opposite processes: the expression 'one world' describes the disappearance of frontiers and differences, whereas with 'inculturation' the emphasis on difference and otherness and the attempt to protect them against levelling are the starting points of the enterprise. In the viewpoint of the first, the world appears as a space which is rapidly becoming more homogeneous and which inflicts the metaphor of the global village on us more and more, whereas in the viewpoint of the inculturation, the world is assumed to be imprinted by various cultures which force Christianity to venture to find its identity among polycultural differences. The following remarks centre around the relationship between these two tendencies.

1. One world—socio-economic

At the presentation of a film award, an actor in the television series Dallas said that the nicest thing about his job was that wherever he went in the world he felt at home, because people watch Dallas everywhere in the world. He was probably not exaggerating. The homogenisation of the world by the mass media is an obvious characteristic of the one world and it does not even escape the eye of the tourist passing through.

It would be insufficient to posit here a neo-colonialism exclusively on the level of consciousness (alienation), which separates mankind from his completely opposite situation in life: the victory of Western civilisation and its 'cult of goods' embraces all areas of society. Thus, a glance at global economic developments demonstrates that the world market has, more and more in the last decades, for the first time, become a fully developed market-place. In his study of 'world market pressures', the economist E. Altvater shows that a rapid expansion of world *trade* was realised, chiefly in the fifties, whereas since the sixties 'as well as the availability of goods, *productive capital* is being internationalised'.[1]

> With the construction of the global monetary system by Bretton Woods in 1944, with the GATT agreement shortly afterwards (even though it was only a poor copy of the free market system foreseen in the Havanna Charter) and the generous aid by the USA to a Western Europe hard hit by the war (Marshall Plan) there arose in effect an *institutional* framework for the internationalisation of the circulation of goods, capital and money. And to the extent to which the process of economic internationalisation progressed, the styles of life and consumption of mankind became universal, as did political models for controlling social conflict. A specific social rationality achieved a global domain and was thus able ... to bring even formerly 'remote' regions under its influence.[2]

On the political level there is also a complex system of international organisations which give structure to world trade (*e.g.*, UNO, International Monetary Fund, World Bank, GATT, etc.). World trade reaches the remotest regions in conjunction with the respective national states and turns them upside down with its logic and its demands. E. Altvater shows this in the example of the Amazon region of Brazil. The 'assessment' of this region also alters the local culture profoundly, even including its fundamental ways of perceiving space and time.[3]

2. One world—ecological

When we speak of one world nowadays, however, the development of world trade is not the central consideration. It is its reverse side—insight into global ecological systems and the threats to nature and thus to the whole of mankind which are brought about by ignorance of these ecological forces. Consciousness, if nothing more, of these problems is at the moment taking control over people's heads and hearts and making real sense to everyone from even the most far-off processes. Thus, solidarity groups in the First World which protest against the threat to the life of Indians posed by the development of the Amazon territory are only successful when they can point out that the destruction of the Amazon rain forest is having catastrophic ecological consequences of global proportions. Sensitivity aroused by these problems sometimes benefits the Indians indirectly.

The consciousness of one world which results from an insight into the ecological context will not be discussed any further, but simply acknowledged as a fact. The important question of how Western civilisation and ecological demands relate to one another can also only be mentioned: many of those engaged in ecological questions see the processes connected with ecological matters to be ultimately incompatible with Western civilisation (and they would include ecology in a one-world-solidarity such as that described in the concluding paragraph). However, it gives one cause for thought that it is without exception the elite members of Western civilisation who are extremely understanding and ready to help with ecological demands.

3. One world without alternatives?

For a long time—particularly in the Third World—the term socialism contained a number of very different concepts, all of which were in agreement that domination by the market-place or the law of values and its rationality ought to be broken, so that life would no longer be permeated and determined by an arbitrary and impersonal economy. Through this channel, the structural preconditions for the preservation and development of a polycultural reality could be created. However, the balance of attempts to establish socialism in this regard are not exactly encouraging. Already in 1980, H. M. Enzensberger, once an avid supporter of basic alternatives, wrote: 'Since the last alternative project in history, Mao Tse-Tung's project, was given up, only one future appears to remain. The peoples of Asia, Africa and Latin America have fallen prey to a universal cargo cult: everything that is new, be it good or bad, comes out of the industrial nations, and everything old has to be sacrificed in its favour.'[4]

Meanwhile, the problem has become clearer. Not only China, but the Soviet Union as well, are involved in an extensive upheaval in which it is not yet clear whether it is leading to a new, more attractive form of socialism or to an increasing assimilation of the economy of these countries to Western models.

Third World countries which have tried to establish a socialist society have all succumbed to great economic difficulties. However one defines the relationship between external pressure and inner problems, it is still universally acknowledged that considerable inner structural problems are partially responsible for these economic crises as well. An important moment in the reaction to these crises at present consists in introducing measures suited to the structure of the world market, but this implies doing without basic alternative methods of development. Looking towards the Third World, H. M. Enzensberger says succinctly: 'There no longer exists an exotic alternative to industrial civilisation.'[5]

Even if one does not see it so clearly and conclusively, one can at least hold on to the fact that something akin to a new evaluation of commercial market elements is taking place. This sharpens the question about the possibility of a polycultural world which not so very long ago was brought under a common denominator with the capitalist world market and consequently romanticised.

4. Social-Theoretical Evaluation of the one world

This poses the question of the relationship of the world-wide triumphal procession of Western civilisation to the non-Western cultures. Will the other cultures in the process of 'modernisation' of the appropriate country maintain their social status or will they be so transformed that, although they appear outwardly to continue to exist, they have renounced every life-giving force that people need? In a recent essay with the title 'Culture and Development', two specialists in developmental matters, U. Menzel and D. Senghaas, present this problem, in the form of the question: Do other cultures hinder 'development'? They neither wish to propagate a renaissance of traditional culture (which would always be artificial), nor a complete westernisation, but they do expect successful development from a combination of innovation in socio-economic areas and cultural consciousness. This may seem like a synthesis, but the very next remark shows how the weights are distributed in this combination: 'However, the more successful such measures are, the more westernised each *economic* structure inevitably becomes and the more the specific cultural identity, over against the economic forces, retreats into the background.'[6]

This points to the evaluation of Western civilisation as that of a totalitarian process on a world scale when worked out in critical theories, particularly by T. W. Adorno and H. Marcuse. Starting out from the Marxist doctrine of values or the problem of reduction, which they broadened into a criticism of reason which is based on the subjugation of nature, they come to the concept of a negative totality, an embracing objective delusion which no longer produces its negation.

As technological universe the advanced industrial society is a *political* universe—the latest step in the realisation of a specific historical *plan*—namely the experience, transformation and organisation of nature as the pure material of domination. While the plan unfolds, it forms the whole universe of speech and action out of intellectual culture. In the medium of the technical, culture, politics and economics are melted down into an omnipresent system which either takes up alternatives into itself or rejects them. (H. Marcuse).[7]

In this line of interpretation there no longer remains a place for the hopes placed in non-European cultures and their potential for an alternative means of forming the universe. Because of a new quality in its infiltration into other cultures, gained above all from technological innovations, Western civilisation seems, nowadays for the first time, to be in a position to draw into its wake even such cultures as have withstood it for centuries, and to rob them of their independence. H. M. Enzensberger formulates this judgment in a very concrete way:

Our idiotic architecture, our supermarkets, our three-bedroom flats, our cosmetics, our television programmes which reach across the entire globe, are only individual moments in an evidently irresistible totality. In our experience of the 'adamantine laws of history' we have had more than one let-down, but the person who watches television is and remains different from people who listen to stories. One thesis of Marxism which no one has yet disproved says that the unleashed productive powers of capitalist industry deal with each stubborn heir, each autonomous 'superstructure'. They are the bulldozers in the history of the world, pushing aside everything that is in the way and levelling all traditional cultures.[8]

In the area of theology, J. B. Metz, for instance, makes this judgment his own, but binds himself—thus both taking up the critical theory and rejecting it—to the theory of the saving power of belief in God, through which the tendency in Western civilisation to destroy the subjective could be withstood.[9]

For example, Metz tries to show that it is in principle possible in the area of religion to break through the movement towards the one-dimensional. The question arising from this is whether this can be considered as coming from religion alone or whether the self-destruction of modernity can be expected in other areas of society equally. This leads to the position which opposes the all pervasive, totalitarian character of Western civilisation.

In the broader realm of critical theory, J. Habermas in particular contradicts this thesis of comprehensive reduction without falling back onto the level reached by the 'older' critical theory. By differentiating between system and lifestyle and similarly between instrumental (or functional) and communicative reason, he tries to demonstrate a 'dual' basis for the process of the development of Western society, thus positing from the very beginning a potential for a logic of communicative reason in the reductive systems-rationality, which lives off a persistent lifestyle. For Habermas, the suitability of this concept can be demonstrated with recourse to the revolt against systems-rationality in the context of the industrial nations themselves, as articulated in the 'New Social Movements' for example. Precisely because we can refer to an inner contradiction in Western civilisation itself, we have the opportunity to think about a wider-reaching life-giving force in non-European cultures even when the countries in question are modernising according to the Western model. In this context as well belong the thoughts, formulated in the area of developmental theory, about a selective takeover of elements of Western civilisation in accordance with the standards of the given culture. (However, it must be pointed out that there are no successful historical examples of such a practice.)[10]

These ideas also deal with the danger of Western civilisation sweeping over other cultures or permeating them. Here too the starting-point is that of the threat to other cultures. Today there is no culture which has been so to speak been 'left in peace'. In other words, the polycultural world is now a historical project.

5. A decision for the global Church

This situation challenges the global Church to take a decision: should it further the process called for by inculturation theology in the direction of a polycultural Christianity or should it try, through an arrangement with Western civilisation, to arrive at universality as the religion to accompany the capitalist victory over the world? The latter suggestion brings the temptation for the Church to continue the practices of the traditional mission, developed in the context of the colonial period, but 'modernised' and finally with worldwide success. It is precisely because Christianity is substantially marked by the culture of European-Western countries that it offers this orientation and one needs to ask whether it too plays a role in the world catechism project.

Out of the many objections against tying Christianity to the 'Western' world, we shall name but two:
1. Western civilisation is definitely not characterised by an identity of

culture and religion, as in other cultures;[11] it is able to separate religion and culture. 'Tolerance' is a moment in its success: it does not lay claim to propogate a particular culture and religion; it is modest and practical in orientation and increasingly strikes roots in all cultures and religions. It would be presumptuous to assume that Christianity could retreat from the process; on the contrary, one can see how Western civilisation attempts to subjugate religion: its potential for liberation and criticism becomes a kind of compensation for the existential wounds inflicted by modernisation and the consolation of coming to terms with the inevitable.[12] Religion and culture thus are becoming an accompaniment to modernisation; they receive their functions from it.

2. The second reason arising from the Church's programme is more important still. The Church's reflection in the last decades (much discussed in this journal) about its specific place on the side of the poor, and of the sacrifices in which it recognises the Lord, puts it on to the side of those who are threatened by Western civilisation or are the victims of the modernisation process (for European Christianity this implies a critical appraisal of its own cultural heritage.) This party-position of the Church, grounded in scripture and tradition, requires that it not first ask for the most efficient means for a global self-propagation, but rather concern itself with the requirements involved in a duty to the poor, the powerless, those on the perimeter and cultural misfits. But the Church can only realise this party-position if it truly lives in the world of those under threat and of the misfits, if it furthers the process of inculturation.

6. Inculturation—between uniformity and contextuality

Thus a fundamental problem arises for the one Church. Christianity is already 'inculturated', first into the Jewish, then into the Hellenistic European-Western civilisation, and it becomes clear on closer examination that there is no Christianity free from inculturation which could be sunk into the respective cultures and there never could be one (a fact which is easily concealed by the field of association of the concept of inculturation).[13] However, this means that there is no 'guarantee of identity', no 'core' which would remain untouched by the process of inculturation. If inculturation is not a trick concept, with the help of which, in a subtle way, membership in the Western Church is to be hurried on,[14] then it entails a great risk for the Church: doing without it, joining the Christian faith in an external way to another culture, or rather understanding inculturation as a practice and formulating faith from within another culture and its structures of rationality, which means from the point of view of the inhabitants of that culture.[15]

This does not lead to a radical contextualism, as is sometimes thought, which considers 'inner' convictions to be incapable of communication, because research into intercultural communication shows that there is in principle a potential for understanding beyond cultural differences. But it also shows to what extent intercultural dialogue is based on the readiness of *both* sides to change. J. Habermas sums it up in this way:

> The fusion of the horizons of interpretation, which, according to Gadamer, is the aim of every process of communication, does not mean an assimilation to 'us', but rather always a convergence of 'our' perspective and 'theirs'—regardless of whether 'they' or 'we' or both sides have more or less to reform their justification practices which were customary up to that point. Even in the most difficult communication process, all parties rely on the common point of reference of a possible consensus, even though each has formulated it from within a different context. This is because concepts like truth, rationality and justice have the same *grammatical* role in *each* linguistic community, although they are differently interpreted and applied according to differing criteria.
>
> Some cultures have certainly exercised the ability to distance themselves from themselves more than others. But all languages offer the possibility of differentiating between what is true and what is considered true. All linguistic practice has the built-in supposition of a common objective world ... From the possibility of linguistic communication we can assume a concept of reason is in position which raises its voice to demand validity both in context-related and in transcendental settings. The validity demanded for propositions and norms transcends space and time, but the demand for validity is made here and now in each case, in particular contexts and is accepted or rejected with actual consequences.[16]

The necessity to make demands for validity which are both context-related and transcendental is described by P. Suess, with regard to specific questions posed by the Church, as the necessity for 'bilingualism' (*bilingüismo*).

> The geographical and cultural areas in which a sign has exactly the same meaning ... are very few. How are we to communicate in a universal church if the ability to communicate its symbols and signs is so restricted? The solution points to a 'bilingualism', through which the 'general language', which secures communication between churches and a 'specific language' which secures communication within the local church.[17]

With the question as to how these two languages are interconnected a whole spectrum of further problems opens which cannot be discussed here.

It is nevertheless time that these questions of intercultural communication will become questions of relevance to the global Church only when Christianity is inculturated into varying cultures, which is not yet the case. Up till now, there have only been attempts to get an impression of how it might work.[18]

7. Solidarity in the one, polycultural world

If the Church, in the face of a globally dangerous association with a Western-dominated world, decides to take the risk of polycultural Christianity, this is also a political option. It is to refuse to model the form of a united church on the pattern of a united world, and at the same time it is to reject a fragmentation of Christianity into a multitude of unconnected cultures. The project of polycultural Christianity in a polycultural world is dependent on a mutual solidarity of the participants, simply because there would be no chance of success otherwise. In the context of thinking about the solidarity of cultures threatened by unification, the concept of 'one world' arises. It intends here to overcome the differences of classification between the First, Second, Third, and Fourth Worlds, while stressing the solidarity of those which are either victims of the modernisation programmes of Western civilisation or in danger of becoming so and of those which, in the context of Western industrial countries follow critical political practices themselves, because they have adopted the 'perspective of the victim'. Their solidarity with the one, polycultural world has a specific character because it does not aim at assimilation one to another but respects difference and otherness and seeks to determine its strength in precisely this way.

From this sort of conception of solidarity, the inner bond between the two great theological themes of 'inculturation' and 'liberation' becomes clear and it is easy to conclude that the passionate debate conducted for some years by the 'Ecumenical Association of Third World Theologians' (EATWOT) as to whether the key concept of a theology based on the Third World ought to be 'inculturation' or 'liberation', could be solved by a convergence of the two.[19] 'Inculturation' and 'liberation' speak for another 'one world' as those concepts whose outline is becoming ever more visible in present reality. It is necessary to differentiate between the 'one world' of Western civilisation and the 'one world' which must not be subjugated to this civilisation. The former 'one world' is a danger, the latter is an opportunity for the global Church.

Translated by Jane Curran

Notes

1. E. Altvater, *Sachzwang Weltmarkt* (Hamburg 1987), p. 228.
2. *Ibid.*, p. 228.
3. *Cf. ibid.*, pp. 104–107; 172–190.
4. H. M. Enzensberger, 'Eurozentrismus wider Willen. Ein politisches Vexierbild', in *idem*, *Politische Brosamen* (Frankfurt 1982), pp.31–52; pp. 47f.
5. *Ibid.*, p. 50. At the same time one should keep in mind that the form of industrialisation successful in the West can certainly not work in all countries because of limits on natural resources.
6. U. Menzel and D. Senghaas, 'Kultur und Entwicklung' in *idem*, *Europas Entwicklung und die Dritte Welt. Eine Bestandsaufnahme* (Frankfurt 1986), pp. 73–86; p. 84.
7. H. Marcuse, *Der Eindimensionale Mensch* (Neuwied/Berlin 1967), pp. 18f.
8. H. M. Enzensberger, *loc. cit.* n. 4, p.41.
9. *Cf.* J. B. Metz, 'Wohin ist Gott, wohin denn der Mensch?' in F.-X. Kaufmann and J. B. Metz, *Zukunftsfähigkeit. Suchbewegung im Christentum* (Freiburg 1987), pp. 124–147.
10. *Cf.* R. Kößler 'Entwicklungs-Optionen zwischen Weltrmarktzusammenhang und Selbstbestimmung. Aspekte eines multifokalen Entwicklungsbegriffs' in *Peripherie (Zeitschrift für Politik und Ökonomie in der Dritten Welt)* 8th Jg. No. 29 (January 1988), pp. 6–23.
11. *Cf.* A. Pieris, *Theologie der Befreiung in Asien. Christentum in Kontext der Armut und der Religionen* (Freiburg 1986), p. 80f. (ET *An Asian Theology of Liberation*, Edinburgh 1988.)
12. *Cf.* the description of the social role of Christianity in H. Lübbe, *Religion nach der Aufklärung* (Graz/Vienna/Cologne 1986).
13. *Cf.* J. B. Metz's contribution to this volume. A detailed theoretical discussion of the concepts used here, such as culture, inculturation, Western civilisation, etc. had to be dispensed with; *cf.* A. Pieris, *op. cit.*, n. 11, esp. pp. 79–91; P. Suess, 'Inculturação. Desafios—caminhos—metas' will appear at the beginning of 1989 in the *Revista Eclesiastica Brasileira*, Petrópolis.
14. A. Pieris, *op. cit.*, n. 11, p. 83 quotes a Buddhist (G. Vitanage), who says about the inculturation movement: 'It appears to be a camouflage which one hides behind in order to break through into the impressive mass of Buddhists and make proselytes out of them, thus using up considerable financial resources of the Church. This process is like a chameleon's tactics; it adapts its colour to suit the surroundings and outwit its prey.'
15. Up till now it was generally the case that to confess Christianity meant a more or less complete break with one's own culture (and religion). A. Pieris stresses the necessity of finding inculturated Christianity precisely through one's own culture and religion. In this context he points to the baptism of Jesus by John, since it was not Jesus who baptised John (as the Church likes to assume for its own image), but rather the other way round. 'In submerging Jesus in the river of an older spirituality he himself stepped out of it and began his new mission. . . . Is it not fear of losing

its identity which prevents the local church from discovering this? Is it not fear of death which prevents it from living?' (*op. cit.*, n. 11, pp. 74f.).

16. J. Habermas, 'Die Einheit der Vernunft in der Vielheit ihrer Stimmen' in *Merkur (Deutsche Zeitschrift für europaisches Denken)* 42nd Jg. Vol. 1 (January 1988), pp. 1–14, pp. 11f.

17. P. Suess, *op. cit.*, n. 13, quoted here according to the manuscript, pp. 31, 42.

18. *Cf.* A. Wagua, 'Erfahrungen im Dialog zwischen dem Christentum und der einheimischen Religion der Kuna' in J. B. Metz and P. Rottländer (eds.) *Lateinamerika und Europa. Dialog der Theologen* (München/Mainz 1988), pp. 135–145; A. Pieris, *Christentum und Buddhismus im Dialog aus der Mitte christlicher Theologie* (Mödling, Österreich 1987), pp. 137–178.

19. The inculturation-liberation debate flared up as a result of the speech made by A. Pieris at the 3rd EATWOT Conference (Asiatic Theological Conference, Colombo/Wennappuwa 1979), *cf.*, Pieris, *op. cit.*, n. 11, pp. 131–160; important contributions to the debate: C. H. Abesamis 'Faith and Life Reflections from the Grassroots in the Philippines' in V. Fabella, *Asia's Struggle for Full Humanity: Towards a Relevant Theology* (New York 1980), pp. 123–139; various contributions to *Logos* 20.1 (March 1981); the resolution appeared at the 5th EATWOT Conference, New Delhi 1981, *cf.*, the speech by A. Pieris, *op. cit.*, n. 11, pp. 161–199, as also in the final document of this conference in *Herausgefordert durch die Armen. Dokumente der Ökumenischen Vereinung von Dritte-Welt Theologen* (Freiburg 1983), pp. 134–135.

PART IV

Concluding Article

Vladimír Benda

World Catechism and the Conciliar Process for Justice, Peace and the Preservation of Creation

WORLD CATECHISM and conciliar process are two projects of our time which, at first glance, have, it is true, nothing in common but are indirectly connected. According to Catholic or Vatican ideas, a world catechism should be a (indeed *the*) centralising model of a 'teaching aid' or a 'document of belief'. But as can be seen from this issue of *Concilium* many theologians and catechists have had difficulties with this. Years ago, B. Häring[1] foresaw that 'biblical' can today still only mean *dicta probantia* to centralised theology and 'liturgical' is incomplete without koinonia and diakonia.

The second project, originally Protestant but now ecumenical, the conciliar process for justice, peace and the preservation of creation, can likewise be understood as something 'global', although here too there are difficulties because it still appears too 'European'.[2]

But the first question is: what does such a process mean? It was Dietrich Bonhoeffer who, in 1934, in the face of the threat of the Nazi regime, called for an ecumenical council to 'proclaim Christ's peace across the raging world'. These are prophetic words, but Christians were not ready for them then and that is why they have not understood them. (Here we see again that Christianity often jumps on a moving train or indeed misses it, because not a few Christians still consider it to be healthier to go on foot through the world because that is what Jesus did. Such ideas are however properly fundamental).

Was Bonhoeffer's idea taken up later by Christians?

I

In 1983 the World Council of Churches held its full meeting in Vancouver, Canada. There it was proposed to convene in 1990 a world conference of churches on justice, peace and the preservation of creation. But presenting a project is one thing, realising it something else. This 'conciliar peace process' too had to experience the gap between theory and practice. The World Council of Churches also invited the Roman Catholic Church to co-operate, but only after a considerable time received a basically positive answer: the Catholic Church will not, indeed, co-operate as an organiser but will co-operate theologically. Indeed, it is already co-operating.

Meanwhile, Catholic and Orthodox theologians drew attention to difficulties with the concept 'ecumenical council' because, in their Churches, this *terminus technicus* has been used for over 1500 years in another sense and has in fact become a concept in canon law and dogma. Protestant, Orthodox and Catholic Christians then agreed on a new term: 'convocation'. But the expression 'conciliar process' continues to be used because it has, in the meantime, taken on a precise content and the concept of 'convocational process' is more of an unusual one.

For Christians in Germany it is important not only that Bonhoeffer initiated this council, but also, and this most particularly so, that it was Carl Friedrich von Weizsäcker, the well-known German physicist and philosopher, who conceived it anew and has become, as it were, the father of the conciliar process. His little book on this, *Time is Pressing* (1986), should be read by everyone. Von Weizsäcker writes there of the demands on today's world and also names the three most important ones as being social justice, political peace and the preservation of creation. He endeavours to classify these demands theologically and to offer practical solutions or a new ethics of peace.

It is interesting for Catholics like us that, for example, B. Häring, whom I have already quoted, spoke years ago of the 'courage for commitment to justice and peace' and testified that 'there are historical moments when non-participation is the greatest failure' and therefore 'our hope at the end of time is only genuine if it urges us to stand up here and now for a better future, a *more just* society and a *more peaceful* world'[3]. In passing, one might add that Catholic Christians are often 'immature' in this respect, when they demand of the 'official Church' that it should always be right at the beginning of a development, that it should be in the vanguard and be the first to recognise the signs of the times. It would be nice if we could one day experience that, but that seems to be an unrealistic idea. Here too I would quote Häring: 'Excessive demands should not be made on the official Church. It is a sign of a lack of a sense of freedom and maturity if one demands of it ready solutions to every new problem . . .'[4]

II

In the meantime a wide variety of committees and organisations have held seminars and conferences, in, for example, Nijmegen (Holland), Budapest (Hungary), Magdeburg and Erfurt (both German Democratic Republic), as well as in Nürnberg, Königstein and Stuttgart (all German Federal Republic). Further sessions were held in Austria and Switzerland, and also in Assisi (Italy) among other places. Even in other world religions the calling of the ecumenical council has been taken to heart.

During Whit week 1989 (15–21 May) the European gathering 'Peace in Justice' will take place in Basle (Switzerland). This will act as a preparation for the 'World Convocation for Peace, Justice and the Preservation of Creation' planned for the 3–12 March 1990 in Seoul (Korea). In Basle, 'the Churches wish to address the politicians on behalf of Christianity in the most binding terms possible on the problems of preserving peace, the creation of more justice between North and South and on the problems of the environment'.[5]

If, in the following, I briefly look at two conferences in the German Federal Republic, that is not only because I live in a neighbouring country and the German Federal Republic has become my theological 'homeland', but also, above all, because Bonhoeffer and von Weizsäcker come from Germany and the process in that country is therefore particularly advanced and precise results have already been achieved.

From 13–16 April 1988 the first phase of the Ecumenical Forum 'Justice, Peace, Preservation of Creation' took place in Königstein. It was organised by the Study Group of Christian Churches in the German Federal Republic and West Berlin (registered society ACK). Of the 120 delegates, 40 came from the Protestant Church, 40 from the Catholic Church and a further 40 from other Churches. The spiritual character of the forum was underlined by church services and daily Bible work. Specialist papers on each of the three aspects provided initial bearings.

The paper on the topic area JUSTICE was given by Professor Erich Geldbach from the Konfessionskundliche Institut in Bensheim. His basic thoughts were as follows: Only God's will, as it is revealed in Jesus Christ, can be the starting point for our deliberations. But to ask about God's will is to ask about God's alternative. God is always a liberator of the oppressed. But the oppressors also belong to the enslaved because through their injustice they enter into self-made slavery. Both oppressors and oppressed therefore need God's liberation and reconciliation.

Asking about God's will means asking about the faithfulness of his covenant which creates a sense of community, about human dignity and finally about God's kingdom. An economic system must be judged according to what it achieves in terms of building a national and international community. From that point of view one can, with the American bishops, describe poverty and unemployment as not only a physical threat to existence but also as a destruction of a person's relation with the community and as a denial of his value in the community.

From that we must draw ethical consequences: the Church, said Geldbach quoting Martin Luther King, cannot be a thermometer in society, that is to say not a measuring instrument, but it must be a thermostat, that is to say a regulating device, and he added: 'Justice is the unit of measurement to which the thermostat is to be set.'

The specialist paper of the topic area PEACE was given by Professor C. F. von Weizsäcker. His main thoughts were as follows: The factual questions facing us are secular, of this world and pressing. The three themes of peace, justice and the preservation of creation are mutually dependent. Humanity in its present phase can then only survive without historically unparalleled catastrophes if and in so far as it succeeds in overcoming the institution of war. This means:

— encouraging disarmament negotiations between the super-powers;
— demanding a ban on the export of weapons;
— promoting peace education.

The specialist paper on the theme CREATION was given by Jean-Pierre Ribaud from the Environment Protection Office on the Council of Europe in Strasburg. His conclusions were as follows:

— human beings and humanity must change their attitude to the environment;
— a change in thought and attitude demands care and wisdom in utilising the earth's resources; energy, water, minerals and oil products can no longer be wasted;
— the Churches must heighten awareness of this; the most recent Papal encyclical *Sollicitudo rei socialis* is, from this point of view, very instructive;
— the new attitudes will then, it is hoped, bring with them a change in human beings which seeks and has its basis in the fundamental values

of the Gospel: humility, respect, active solidarity and commitment amongst others. Only in this way can human beings do justice to the task which God has set them as custodians of His creation.[6]

As a result of the Königstein forum, there was considerable dissatisfaction with the theses worked out there; this was expressed right across Germany on a Church basis in hundreds of discussions and working sessions in parishes and groups from Christian Churches. Some of the theses were described as 'superficial and wishy-washy'; the Ecumenical Initiative 'One World' in Cologne spoke of 'empty husks of no consequence for our Christian action'. The work-group 'Peace II' in particular, which had been concerned with the overcoming of deterrence, was heavily criticised, not least because its members—amongst whom were four high-ranking officers of the West German Army, professors of political science, pacifists and representatives of the group 'Holy Orders for Peace'—were irreconcilably opposed to one another. There were 800 submissions on the Königstein theses to the forum's offices in Hanover which had to be taken into account in preparing for the Second Ecumenical Forum. This took place in Stuttgart from 20–22 October 1988 and was again organised by the Study Group of Christian Churches (ACK).

Here too the conflicts between the differing schools of thought came into the open, but precise and improved formulations were reached on war, nuclear deterrence and the refusal to do military service. On the last day more than four dozen motions for change and a draft resolution of over 70 pages were discussed and voted on with a large majority in agreement. All Christian Churches in the German Federal Republic have *unanimously* taken up a position on the questions of justice, peace and the preservation of creation—an historic event, which fact and consequences politicians will be unable to escape.[7]

III

I am writing this rather incomplete information about the conciliar process only two weeks after the Stuttgart forum. In the meantime I have received the first draft of a working document for the already mentioned European Ecumenical Gathering in Basle; this document is based on the discussions of the common planning group of the Conference of European Churches (CEC) and the Council of the European Conference of Bishops (Concilium Conferentiarum Episcopalium Europae—CCEE). With this, Christians and Churches in all European countries and at all levels are to be invited to take part in the formulation of a Christian answer to the crisis and to the prospects for today's world. The organisers understand

the Basle gathering as an act of obedience before God and therefore pray
for the ability to hear the Holy Spirit and to obey it. They confess the guilt
of European Churches and Christians in the conquest, colonisation,
economic exploitation and cultural domination of the Third World and
perceive their share of the responsibility in the resulting global crisis. They
refer to the image of the 'European house', a part of the global village, and
to the necessity that we, who are such close neighbours in Europe, must
find a way of living together in the same space, in spite of the fact of
different nations, political systems and world views. I will look again at
this in Section IV.

The working document, to be followed by a second draft, contains a
wealth of stimulating ideas which cannot be gone into here. I do however
recommend all those interested to request further materials from:

'Frieden in Gerechtigkeit'
Postfach
CH—4021 Basel

IV

Of what use is all this information about the conciliar process in an
edition of Conciluum concerned with the problem of world catechism
and why should they be presented by a Czech of all people? On this I
would make the following remarks:

The image of the 'European house', which has, in the meantime, become
widely known and which takes account of the plurality of Europe and at
the same time underlines our duty to this common if divided house, is
precisely for Christians in Eastern Europe a hope for the future. We too
would like to co-operate in realising justice and peace as well as the
preservation of creation. Because we live in different political systems, we
must, so that our voice is heard at all, sometimes carry out our work for
peace together with non-Christian groups (Marxists, atheists) with whom
we have not only been living together for more than 40 years, but with
whom for many years we have also been in dialogue (not in continual
confrontation). Should we continue in silence or should we, at least in this
way, raise our voices in this European house, even if we run the danger of
sometimes been misunderstood by Christians in Western Europe and of
being judged as 'collaborators'? The conciliar process allows us to hope for
more understanding for our situation among our fellow European
Christians, and that is why we view it with so much interest and in Christian
hope.

If I may consider one final aspect: world catechism and conciliar process are certainly quite different projects, but both typical of our time. On the one hand we have a concentration on the one doctrine, even the one catechism, as if today a real polycentric inculturation no longer existed; on the other hand we see an authentic Christian decentralisation of service (of services) to mankind today, although we will not for a long time be finished, in ecumenical terms, with the biblical saying 'one faith, one baptism, one Lord'. Both methods have advantages and disadvantages, but one thing is sure: for ecumenism, for service to the world, there can and should not be today any 'dogmatising'. We find ourselves in a situation in which we must allow 'processes' free play, and in fact not only 'immanent processes of the Trinity' (which surely are and remain the very basis of all activities), but also all 'economic world processes' which should be and will always remain ecumenical-conciliar. In the conciliar process, with which we have been concerned, there is a secular analogy to perichoresis: the *just* Father, the eternal, ultimate source of the universe; the Son who has personally become and remains our *peace*; the Holy Ghost who at every moment renews, inspires and *preserves* all things.

Translated by Gordon Wood

Notes

1. *Frei in Christus* (1979), I, 95.
2. *Cf.*, criticism from the Third World in *Publik Forum*, 17/88, 8 'Europas Enge sprengen'.
3. *Op. cit.*, n. 1, pp. 105, 164.
4. *Ibid.*, p. 169.
5. Protestant News Service, West Germany.
6. *Documentation* (Frankfurt am Main), Nos. 19–20/88.
7. *Cf.*, Frank S. Rödiger in *Das Deutsche Allgemeine Sonntagsblatt*, 44/88.

Contributors

EMILIO ALBERICH was born in Algeciras (Spain) in 1933. He studied philosophy and theology at the Pontifical Salesian Atheneum in Turin. Since 1964, he has been Professor of Catechetics at the Pontifical Salesian University in Rome. He is currently Director of the Catechetical Institute in the Faculty of the Science of Education at the same university. His main publications include: *Orientamenti attuali della catechesi* (Turin 1971); *Natura e compiti di una catechesi moderna* (Turin 1972); *Catechesi e prassi ecclesiale* (Turin 1982); *A catequese na Igreja de hoje* (Sâo Paulo 1983).

VLADIMÍR BENDA was born in 1927 in Czechoslovakia; consecrated priest in Prague in 1950; then active in spiritual welfare work. In 1962 he gained his doctorate at the Theological Faculty in Leitmeritz with a dissertation on the theme 'Priesthood in the Old and New Testaments'; in 1974 he received a post-doctoral lecturing qualification, also in Leitmeritz, with a paper on Karl Rahner's study 'The future of the Church has already begun'. He has been a lecturer in the Theologicl Faculty in Leitmeritz (Basic Theology Course and Practical Theology) for 12 years. His publications include: *Tagebuch des kleinen Joseph* [Children's Catechism] 1968; *Suchen* [Questions about the meaning of life] 1988; *Finden* [Theological answers] appearing 1989; *Theologische Systematik* [Dictionary relating to the interpretation of history and divine grace] appearing 1989.

RAYMOND BRODEUR was born in Quebec in 1946. He holds a joint doctorate in Science of Religions and Theology from the Sorbonne and the Institut Catholique in Paris. He teaches catechesis at Laval University in Quebec, where he also leads the group responsible for research into catechism production. He has published articles in several specialist reviews and is co-editor of *Une inconnue de l'histoire de la culture: La production des catéchismes en Amérique française* (1986) and *Les études pastorales: une discipline scientifique?* (1987).

HERMANN HÄRING was born in 1937, and studied theology in Munich and Tübingen. From 1969 to 1980 he was on the staff of the Institute for Ecumenical Research in Tübingen, and since 1980 has been Professor of Dogmatic Theology at the Catholic University in Nijmegen.

His writings include dissertations on Church and kerygma, and on the power of evil, and articles on ecclesiology, christology, etc.

JEAN JONCHERAY is a priest in the diocese of Angers (France) and teaches in the Theology and Religious Science Research Unit at the Institut Catholique in Paris. Since 1984 he has been Director of the Institute Supérieur de Pastorale Catéchétique.

His numerous publications on the relationship of catechesis to its socio-cultural context include both contemporary and historical aspects of the subject.

BERARD MARTHALER, OFM Conv. holds doctorates in theology (Rome) and history (University of Minnesota). He is Professor of Religion and Religious Education at the Catholic University of America, Washington, DC where he has been a member of the Faculty since 1963. Fr Marthaler is executive editor of *The Living Light*, an interdisciplinary review of Catholic religious education, catechesis and pastoral ministry, published under the auspices of the United States Catholic Conference.

JOHANN-BAPTIST METZ was born in 1928 in Auerbach (Bavaria), was ordained priest in 1954, holds doctorates in philosophy and theology, and is currently Professor of Fundamental Theology in the University of Münster. His publications include: *Armut im Geiste* (1962); *Christliche Anthropozentrik* (1962); *Zur Theologie der Welt*, 1968 (ET Theology of the World, 1969); *Reform und Gegenreformation heute* (1969); *Kirche im Prozeß der Aufklärung* (1970); *Die Theologie in der interdisziplinären Forschung* (1971); *Leidensgeschichte* (1973); *Unsere Hoffnung* (1975); *Zeit der Orden? Zur Mystik und Politik der Nachfolge* (1977); *Glaube in Geschichte und Gesellschaft*, 1977 (ET Faith in History and Society, 1980) *Gott nach Auschwitz* (1979); *Jenseits bürgerlicher Religion* (1980); *Unterbrechungen* (1981); *Die Theologie der Befreiung—Hoffnung oder Gefahr für die Kirche?* (1986); *Zukunftsfähigkeit. Suchbewegungen im Christentum* (1987); *Lateinamerika und Europa: Dialog der Theologen* (1988).

PETER ROTTLÄNDER was born 1953 in Gummersbach (West Germany). He studied theology in Bonn and Münster. He was theology tutor at a Junior College 1979–83; Academic Assistant at the Fundamental Theology Department in the University of Münster 1983–9. At present he is working at Misereor, Aachen.

He has published various articles in books and journals, and edited *Theologie der Befreiung und Marxismus* (Münster 1986); and (with J.-B. Metz) *Lateinamerika und Europa. Dialog der Theologen* (München/Mainz 1988).

PETER SCHINELLER, SJ was born in 1939 in New York City and ordained a priest in 1970. He holds a doctorate in systematic theology from the University of Chicago. From 1981–6 he was Dean and Lecturer at the Catholic Institute of West Africa, Port Harcourt, Nigeria. After teaching at Weston School of Theology, Cambridge, MA for three years, he returns to Africa in 1989.

He has published in numerous journals in the USA and Nigeria. Among his writings are a monograph on *The Newer Approaches to Christology and their use in the Spiritual Exercises* (St. Louis 1980) and a forthcoming volume on inculturation.

DAVID TRACY was born 1939 in Yonkers, New York. He is a priest of the diocese of Bridgeport, Connecticut, and a doctor of theology of the Gregorian University, Rome. He is Distinguished Service Professor of Theology at the Divinity School of Chicago University. He is the author of *The Achievement of Bernard Lonergan* (1970); *Blessed Rage for Order: New Pluralism in Theology* (1975), *The Analogical Imagination* (1980); and *Plurality and Ambiguity* (1986). He contributes to several reviews and is editor of the *Journal of Religion* and of the *Religious Studies Review*.

JÜRGEN WERBICK was born in Aschaffenburg in 1946. He studied philosophy and theology at Mainz, Munich and Zürich. He gained his doctorate under H. Fries in 1973, and in 1981 received his *Habilitation* for fundamental and ecumenical theology. Since then he has been Professor of Systematic Theology at the University and Polytechnic of Siegen. He has contributed many articles to symposia and periodicals. His publications include: *Die Aporetik des Ethischen und der christliche Glaube* (1976); *Glaube im Kontext* (²1988); *Schulderfahrung und Bußsakrament* (1985); and *Glaubenlernen aus Erfahrung* (1989).

CONCILIUM

1. (Vol. 1 No. 1) **Dogma.** Ed. Edward Schillebeeckx. 86pp.
2. (Vol. 2 No. 1) **Liturgy.** Ed. Johannes Wagner. 100pp.
3. (Vol. 3 No. 1) **Pastoral.** Ed. Karl Rahner. 104pp.
4. (Vol. 4 No. 1) **Ecumenism.** Hans Küng. 108pp.
5. (Vol. 5 No. 1) **Moral Theology.** Ed. Franz Bockle. 98pp.
6. (Vol. 6 No. 1) **Church and World.** Ed. Johannes Baptist Metz. 92pp.
7. (Vol. 7 No. 1) **Church History.** Roger Aubert. 92pp.
8. (Vol. 8 No. 1) **Canon Law.** Ed. Teodoro Jimenez Urresti and Neophytos Edelby. 96pp.
9. (Vol. 9 No. 1) **Spirituality.** Ed. Christian Duquoc. 88pp.
10. (Vol. 10 No. 1) **Scripture.** Ed. Pierre Benoit and Roland Murphy. 92pp.
11. (Vol. 1 No. 2) **Dogma.** Ed. Edward Shillebeeckx. 88pp.
12. (Vol. 2 No. 2) **Liturgy.** Ed. Johannes Wagner. 88pp.
13. (Vol. 3 No. 2) **Pastoral.** Ed. Karl Rahner. 84pp.
14. (Vol. 4 No. 2) **Ecumenism.** Ed. Hans Küng. 96pp.
15. (Vol. 5 No. 2) **Moral Theology.** Ed. Franz Bockle. 88pp.
16. (Vol. 6 No. 2) **Church and World.** Ed. Johannes Baptist Metz. 84pp.
17. (Vol. 7 No. 2) **Church History.** Ed. Roger Aubert. 96pp.
18. (Vol. 8 No. 2) **Religious Freedom.** Ed. Neophytos Edelby and Teodoro Jimenez Urresti. 96pp.
19. (Vol. 9 No. 2) **Religionless Christianity?** Ed. Christian Duquoc. 96pp.
20. (Vol. 10 No. 2) **The Bible and Tradition.** Ed. Pierre Benoit and Roland E. Murphy. 96pp.
21. (Vol. 1 No. 3) **Revelation and Dogma.** Ed. Edward Schillebeeckx. 88pp.
22. (Vol. 2 No. 3) **Adult Baptism and Initiation.** Ed. Johannes Wagner. 96pp.
23. (Vol. 3 No. 3) **Atheism and Indifference.** Ed. Karl Rahner. 92pp.
24. (Vol. 4 No. 3) **The Debate on the Sacraments.** Ed. Hans Küng. 92pp.
25. (Vol. 5 No. 3) **Morality, Progress and History.** Ed. Franz Bockle. 84pp.
26. (Vol. 6 No. 3) **Evolution.** Ed. Johannes Baptist Metz. 88pp.
27. (Vol. 7 No. 3) **Church History.** Ed. Roger Aubert. 92pp.
28. (Vol. 8 No. 3) **Canon Law— Theology and Renewal.** Ed. Neophytos Edelby and Teodoro Jimenez Urresti. 92pp.
29. (Vol. 9 No. 3) **Spirituality and Politics.** Ed. Christian Duquoc. 84pp.
30. (Vol. 10 No. 3) **The Value of the Old Testament.** Ed. Pierre Benoit and Roland Murphy. 92pp.
31. (Vol. 1 No. 4) **Man, World and Sacrament.** Ed. Edward Schillebeeckx. 84pp.
32. (Vol. 2 No. 4) **Death and Burial: Theology and Liturgy.** Ed. Johannes Wagner. 88pp.

33. (Vol. 3 No. 4) **Preaching the Word of God.** Ed. Karl Rahner. 96pp.
34. (Vol. 4 No. 4) **Apostolic by Succession?** Ed. Hans Küng. 96pp.
35. (Vol. 5 No. 4) **The Church and Social Morality.** Ed. Franz Bockle. 92pp.
36. (Vol. 6 No. 4) **Faith and the World of Politics.** Ed. Johannes Baptist Metz. 96pp.
37. (Vol. 7 No. 4) **Prophecy.** Ed. Roger Aubert. 80pp.
38. (Vol. 8 No. 4) **Order and the Sacraments.** Ed. Neophytos Edelby and Teodoro Jimenez Urresti. 96pp.
39. (Vol. 9 No. 4) **Christian Life and Eschatology.** Ed. Christian Duquoc. 94pp.
40. (Vol. 10 No. 4) **The Eucharist: Celebrating the Presence of the Lord.** Ed. Pierre Benoit and Roland Murphy. 88pp.
41. (Vol. 1 No. 5) **Dogma.** Ed. Edward Schillebeeckx. 84pp.
42. (Vol. 2 No. 5) **The Future of the Liturgy.** Ed. Johannes Wagner. 92pp.
43. (Vol. 3 No. 5) **The Ministry and Life of Priests Today.** Ed. Karl Rahner. 104pp.
44. (Vol. 4 No. 5) **Courage Needed.** Ed. Hans Küng. 92pp.
45. (Vol. 5 No. 5) **Profession and Responsibility in Society.** Ed. Franz Bockle. 84pp.
46. (Vol. 6 No. 5) **Fundamental Theology.** Ed. Johannes Baptist Metz. 84pp.
47. (Vol. 7 No. 5) **Sacralization in the History of the Church.** Ed. Roger Aubert. 80pp.
48. (Vol. 8 No. 5) **The Dynamism of Canon Law.** Ed. Neophytos Edelby and Teodoro Jimenez Urresti. 92pp.
49. (Vol. 9 No. 5) **An Anxious Society Looks to the Gospel.** Ed. Christian Duquoc. 80pp.
50. (Vol. 10 No. 5) **The Presence and Absence of God.** Ed. Pierre Benoit and Roland Murphy. 88pp.
51. (Vol. 1 No. 6) **Tension between Church and Faith.** Ed. Edward Schillebeeckx. 156pp.
52. (Vol. 2 No. 6) **Prayer and Community.** Ed. Herman Schmidt. 156pp.
53. (Vol. 3 No. 6) **Catechetics for the Future.** Ed. Alois Müller. 168pp.
54. (Vol. 4 No. 6) **Post-Ecumenical Christianity.** Ed. Hans Küng. 168pp.
55. (Vol. 5 No. 6) **The Future of Marriage as Institution.** Ed. Franz Bockle. 180pp.
56. (Vol. 6 No. 6) **Moral Evil Under Challenge.** Ed. Johannes Baptist Metz. 160pp.
57. (Vol. 7 No. 6) **Church History at a Turning Point.** Ed. Roger Aubert. 160pp.
58. (Vol. 8 No. 6) **Structures of the Church's Presence in the World of Today.** Ed. Teodoro Jimenez Urresti. 160pp.
59. (Vol. 9 No. 6) **Hope.** Ed. Christian Duquoc. 160pp.
60. (Vol. 10 No. 6) **Immortality and Resurrection.** Ed. Pierre Benoit and Roland Murphy. 160pp.

61. (Vol. 1 No. 7) **The Sacramental Administration of Reconciliation.** Ed. Edward Schillebeeckx. 160pp
62. (Vol. 2 No. 7) **Worship of Christian Man Today.** Ed. Herman Schmidt. 156pp.
63. (Vol. 3 No. 7) **Democratization of the Church.** Ed. Alois Müller. 160pp.
64. (Vol. 4 No. 7) **The Petrine Ministry in the Church.** Ed. Hans Küng. 160pp.
65. (Vol. 5 No. 7) **The Manipulation of Man.** Ed. Franz Bockle. 144pp.
66. (Vol. 6 No. 7) **Fundamental Theology in the Church.** Ed. Johannes Baptist Metz. 156pp.
67. (Vol. 7 No. 7) **The Self-Understanding of the Church.** Ed. Roger Aubert. 144pp.
68. (Vol. 8 No. 7) **Contestation in the Church.** Ed. Teodoro Jimenez Urresti. 152pp.
69. (Vol. 9 No. 7) **Spirituality, Public or Private?** Ed. Christian Duquoc 156pp.
70. (Vol. 10 No. 7) **Theology, Exegesis and Proclamation.** Ed. Roland Murphy. 144pp.
71. (Vol. 1 No. 8) **The Bishop and the Unity of the Church.** Ed. Edward Schillebeeckx. 156pp.
72. (Vol. 2 No. 8) **Liturgy and the Ministry.** Ed. Herman Schmidt. 160pp.
73. (Vol. 3 No. 8) **Reform of the Church.** Ed. Alois Müller and Norbert Greinacher. 152pp.
74. (Vol. 4 No. 8) **Mutual Recognition of Ecclesial Ministries?** Ed. Hans Küng and Walter Kasper. 152pp.
75. (Vol. 5 No. 8) **Man in a New Society.** Ed. Franz Bockle. 160pp
76. (Vol. 6 No. 8) **The God Question.** Ed. Johannes Baptist Metz. 156pp.
77. (Vol. 7 No. 8) **Election-Consensus Reception.** Ed. Giuseppe Alberigo and Anton Weiler. 156pp.
78. (Vol. 8 No. 8) **Celibacy of the Catholic Priest.** Ed. William Bassett and Peter Huizing. 160pp
79. (Vol. 9 No. 8) **Prayer.** Ed. Christian Duquoc and Claude Geffré. 126pp.
80. (Vol. 10 No. 8) **Ministries in the Church.** Ed. Bas van Iersel and Roland Murphy. 152pp.
81. **The Persistence of Religion.** Ed. Andrew Greeley and Gregory Baum. 0 8164 2537 X 168pp.
82. **Liturgical Experience of Faith.** Ed Herman Schmidt and David Power. 0 8164 2538 8 144pp.
83. **Truth and Certainty.** Ed. Edward Schillebeeckx and Bas van Iersel. 0 8164 2539 6 144pp.
84. **Political Commitment and Christian Community.** Ed. Alois Müller and Norbert Greinacher. 0 8164 2540 X 156pp.
85. **The Crisis of Religious Language.** Ed. Johannes Baptist Metz and Jean-Pierre Jossua. 0 8164 2541 8 144pp.
86. **Humanism and Christianity.** Ed. Claude Geffré. 0 8164 2542 6 144pp.
87. **The Future of Christian Marriage** Ed. William Bassett and Peter Huizing. 0 8164 2575 2.

88. **Polarization in the Church.** Ed. Hans Küng and Walter Kasper. 0 8164 2572 8 156pp.
89. **Spiritual Revivals.** Ed. Christian Duquoc and Casiano Floristán. 0 8164 2573 6 156pp.
90. **Power and the Word of God.** Ed. Franz Bockle and Jacques Marie Pohier. 0 8164 2574 4 156pp.
91. **The Church as Institution.** Ed. Gregory Baum and Andrew Greeley. 0 8164 2575 2 168pp.
92. **Politics and Liturgy.** Ed. Herman Schmidt and David Power. 0 8164 2576 0 156pp.
93. **Jesus Christ and Human Freedom.** Ed. Edward Schillebeeckx and Bas van Iersel. 0 8164 2577 9 168pp.
94. **The Experience of Dying.** Ed. Norbert Greinacher and Alois Müller. 0 8164 2578 7 156pp.
95. **Theology of Joy.** Ed. Johannes Baptist Metz and Jean-Pierre Jossua. 0 8164 2579 5 164pp.
96. **The Mystical and Political Dimension of the Christian Faith.** Ed. Claude Geffré and Gustavo Guttierez. 0 8164 2580 9 168pp.
97. **The Future of the Religious Life.** Ed. Peter Huizing and William Bassett. 0 8164 2094 7 96pp.
98. **Christians and Jews.** Ed. Hans Küng and Walter Kasper. 0 8164 2095 5 96pp.
99. **Experience of the Spirit.** Ed. Peter Huizing and William Bassett. 0 8164 2096 3 144pp.
100. **Sexuality in Contemporary Catholicism.** Ed. Franz Bockle and Jacques Marie Pohier. 0 8164 2097 1 126pp.
101. **Ethnicity.** Ed. Andrew Greeley and Gregory Baum. 0 8164 2145 5 120pp.
102. **Liturgy and Cultural Religious Traditions.** Ed. Herman Schmidt and David Power. 0 8164 2146 2 120pp.
103. **A Personal God?** Ed. Edward Schillebeeckx and Bas van Iersel. 0 8164 2149 8 142pp.
104. **The Poor and the Church.** Ed. Norbert Greinacher and Alois Müller. 0 8164 2147 1 128pp.
105. **Christianity and Socialism.** Ed. Johannes Baptist Metz and Jean-Pierre Jossua. 0 8164 2148 X 144pp.
106. **The Churches of Africa: Future Prospects.** Ed. Claude Geffré and Bertrand Luneau. 0 8164 2150 1 128pp.
107. **Judgement in the Church.** William Bassett and Peter Huizing. 0 8164 2166 8 128pp.
108. **Why Did God Make Me?** Ed. Hans Küng and Jürgen Moltmann. 0 8164 2167 6 112pp.
109. **Charisms in the Church.** Ed. Christian Duquoc and Casiano Floristán. 0 8164 2168 4 128pp.
110. **Moral Formation and Christianity.** Ed. Franz Bockle and Jacques Marie Pohier. 0 8164 2169 2 120pp.
111. **Communication in the Church.** Ed. Gregory Baum and Andrew Greeley. 0 8164 2170 6 126pp.

112. **Liturgy and Human Passage.** Ed. David Power and Luis Maldonado. 0 8164 2608 2 136pp.
113. **Revelation and Experience.** Ed. Edward Schillebeeckx and Bas van Iersel. 0 8164 2609 0 134pp.
114. **Evangelization in the World Today.** Ed. Norbert Greinacher and Alois Müller. 0 8164 2610 4 136pp.
115. **Doing Theology in New Places.** Ed. Jean-Pierre Jossua and Johannes Baptist Metz. 0 8164 2611 2 120pp.
116. **Buddhism and Christianity.** Ed. Claude Geffré and Mariasusai Dhavamony. 0 8164 2612 0 136pp.
117. **The Finances of the Church.** Ed. William Bassett and Peter Huizing. 0 8164 2197 8 160pp.
118. **An Ecumenical Confession of Faith?** Ed. Hans Küng and Jürgen Moltmann. 0 8164 2198 6 136pp.
119. **Discernment of the Spirit and of Spirits.** Ed. Casiano Floristán and Christian Duquoc. 0 8164 2199 4 136pp.
120. **The Death Penalty and Torture.** Ed. Franz Bockle and Jacques Marie Pohier. 0 8164 2200 1 136pp.
121. **The Family in Crisis or in Transition.** Ed. Andrew Greeley. 0 567 30001 3 128pp.
122. **Structures of Initiation in Crisis.** Ed. Luis Maldonado and David Power. 0 567 30002 1 128pp.
123. **Heaven.** Ed. Bas van Iersel and Edward Schillebeeckx. 0 567 30003 X 120pp.
124. **The Church and the Rights of Man.** Ed. Alois Müller and Norbert Greinacher. 0 567 30004 8 140pp.
125. **Christianity and the Bourgeoisie.** Ed. Johannes Baptist Metz. 0 567 30005 6 144pp.
126. **China as a Challenge to the Church.** Ed. Claude Geffré and Joseph Spae. 0 567 30006 4 136pp.
127. **The Roman Curia and the Communion of Churches.** Ed. Peter Huizing and Knut Walf. 0 567 30007 2 144pp.
128. **Conflicts about the Holy Spirit.** Ed. Hans Küng and Jürgen Moltmann. 0 567 30008 0 144pp.
129. **Models of Holiness.** Ed. Christian Duquoc and Casiano Floristán. 0 567 30009 9 128pp.
130. **The Dignity of the Despised of the Earth.** Ed. Jacques Marie Pohier and Dietmar Mieth. 0 567 30010 2 144pp.
131. **Work and Religion.** Ed. Gregory Baum. 0 567 30011 0 148pp.
132. **Symbol and Art in Worship.** Ed. Luis Maldonado and David Power. 0 567 30012 9 136pp.
133. **Right of the Community to a Priest.** Ed. Edward Schillebeeckx and Johannes Baptist Metz. 0 567 30013 7 148pp.
134. **Women in a Men's Church.** Virgil Elizondo and Norbert Greinacher. 0 567 30014 5 144pp.
135. **True and False Universality of Christianity.** Ed. Claude Geffré and Jean-Pierre Jossua. 0 567 30015 3 138pp.

136. **What is Religion? An Inquiry for Christian Theology.** Ed. Mircea Eliade and David Tracy. 0 567 30016 1 98pp.
137. **Electing our Own Bishops.** Ed. Peter Huizing and Knut Walf. 0 567 30017 X 112pp.
138. **Conflicting Ways of Interpreting the Bible.** Ed. Hans Küng and Jürgen Moltmann. 0 567 30018 8 112pp.
139. **Christian Obedience.** Ed. Casiano Floristán and Christian Duquoc. 0 567 30019 6 96pp.
140. **Christian Ethics and Economics: the North-South Conflict.** Ed. Dietmar Mieth and Jacques Marie Pohier. 0 567 30020 X 128pp.
141. **Neo-Conservatism: Social and Religious Phenomenon.** Ed. Gregory Baum and John Coleman. 0 567 30021 8.
142. **The Times of Celebration.** Ed. David Power and Mary Collins. 0 567 30022 6.
143. **God as Father.** Ed. Edward Schillebeeckx and Johannes Baptist Metz. 0 567 30023 4.
144. **Tensions Between the Churches of the First World and the Third World.** Ed. Virgil Elizondo and Norbert Greinacher. 0 567 30024 2.
145. **Nietzsche and Christianity.** Ed. Claude Geffré and Jean-Pierre Jossua. 0 567 30025 0.
146. **Where Does the Church Stand?** Ed. Giuseppe Alberigo. 0 567 30026 9.
147. **The Revised Code of Canon Law: a Missed Opportunity?** Ed. Peter Huizing and Knut Walf. 0 567 30027 7.
148. **Who Has the Say in the Church?** Ed. Hans Küng and Jürgen Moltmann. 0 567 30028 5.
149. **Francis of Assisi Today.** Ed. Casiano Floristán and Christian Duquoc. 0 567 30029 3.
150. **Christian Ethics: Uniformity, Universality, Pluralism.** Ed. Jacques Pohier and Dietmar Mieth. 0 567 30030 7.
151. **The Church and Racism.** Ed. Gregory Baum and John Coleman. 0 567 30031 5.
152. **Can we always celebrate the Eucharist?** Ed. Mary Collins and David Power. 0 567 30032 3.
153. **Jesus, Son of God?** Ed. Edward Schillebeeckx and Johannes-Baptist Metz. 0 567 30033 1.
154. **Religion and Churches in Eastern Europe.** Ed. Virgil ELizondo and Norbert Greinacher. 0 567 30034 X.
155. **'The Human', Criterion of Christian Existence?** Ed. Claude Geffré and Jean-Pierre Jossua. 0 567 30035 8.
156. **The Challenge of Psychology to Faith.** Ed. Steven Kepnes (Guest Editor) and David Tracy. 0 567 30036 6.
157. **May Church Ministers be Politicians?** Ed. Peter Huizing and Knut Walf. 0 567 30037 4.
158. **The Right to Dissent.** Ed. Hans Küng and Jürgen Moltmann. 0 567 30038 2.

CONCILIUM

CONCILIUM 1988

All back issues are still in print: available from bookshops or direct from the publishers (£5.95/US$11.95/Can$12.75 excluding postage and packing).

T & T CLARK LTD, 59 GEORGE STREET
EDINBURGH EH2 2LQ, SCOTLAND